The ultimate

INSTANT

POT

COOKBOOK 2019

550 Deliciously Simple Recipes for
Your Electric Pressure cooker

BY

Alexander Bedria

Copyright © 2017; By Alexander bedria

All rights reserved. This book is copyright protected and it's for personal use only. No part of this publication may be reproduced, distributed, or transmitted in any form or by any means, including photocopying, recording, or other electronic or mechanical methods, without the prior written permission of the publisher, except in the case of brief quotations embodied in critical reviews and certain other non-commercial uses permitted by copyright law. This document is geared towards providing substantial and reliable information in regards to the topics covered.

Disclaimer

Please note, the information written in this book, are for educational and entertainment purposes only. Strenuous efforts have been made to provide accurate, up to date and reliable complete information in this book. All recommendations are made without guarantee on the part of the author and publisher. By reading this document, the reader agrees that under no circumstances are we responsible for any losses, direct or indirect, which are incurred as a result of the use of the information contained in this document, including but not limited to errors, omissions or inaccuracies.

Table of Contents

INTRODUCTION

Welcome to Instant Pot cookbook

New to the Instant pot? Congratulations and welcome aboard to the world of fast and easy cooking. If you have cooked with a Pressure Cooker, then you will be familiar with this kitchen appliance. Pressure cooking is an amazing way to cook. The Instant Pot enables you to cook a wide variety of dishes including meat, fish, soup, grain, poultry, beans, cakes, yogurt and vegetables etc. And getting to pressure cook with an Electric Pressure Cooker is even more interesting.

The Instant Pot serves as a multi-use programmable appliance that can help create easy, fast and delicious recipes with the ability to apply different cooking settings all in one pot. With it, you don't have to worry about not having time for homemade meals. As everything is fast, and convenient that in minutes, your healthy, tasty meal is ready to be served.

In this cookbook, **the ultimate Instant Pot cookbook 2019: 550 deliciously simple recipes for your Electric Pressure Cooker**, you will find collection of easy and modern delicious recipes with detailed Instructions that will guide and help you start your pressure-cooking journey on a good note. The vast majority of the recipes in this cookbook can be prepared and served in less than 45 minutes. Each recipe is written with the exact preparation time, cooking time, overall time, cooking instructions and ingredients required to prepare the dishes. This cookbook is meant for beginners & advanced users, so the cooking instructions is written in easy format for newbies to comprehend.

CHAPTER 1: Benefits of Using an Instant Pot

1. **Saving Time & Energy:** Instant Pot are extremely quick at cooking that they diminish your cooking time impressively sparing you some time for different things that may require your consideration. The Instant Pot cook foods much faster than any other methods of cooking. The Electric Pressure Cooker can reduce cooking time by up to 70% when compared with any other traditional methods of cooking. Cooking with an Instant Pot requires less water used in cooking and much less energy is required thereby saving up to 70% of energy comparing with boiling, steaming, and slow cooking.

2. **Preserving Nutrients & Cook Tasty Food:** Pressure cooking ensures that heat is evenly and quickly distributed while cooking. The vitamins and minerals will not be dissolved or leached away by water. Because the food is surrounded with the steam, the foods will not be oxidized by air exposure at heat, so asparagus, lentil, broccoli, artichoke, and other veggies retain their bright green colors and phytochemicals. It will also enable the food to retains its original flavor. Scientific studies have proved that pressure cooking is the best method for retaining the vitamins and minerals of the food that your body needs.

3. **Eliminating Harmful Micro-Organisms in Food:** Instant Pot cooks Foods at a temperature above the boiling point of water, killing almost all harmful living micro-organisms such as bacteria, fungi, and viruses. It helps to destroy all harmful micro-organisms that are toxic to your health.

4. **Helps Boost Digestibility of Foods:** Pressure cooking helps to boost the digestibility of the foods you cook. I believe you must have heard, "You are what you eat." But actually, you are what you absorb from your food. Boosting the digestibility of your food will maximize the nutritional value to your body. Pressure cooking your food makes the toughest meats moist and tender, which makes the food to digest easily.

5. **Ease and Convenience:** The simplicity and comfort you get from cooking with the Instant Pot are so colossal. With the hit of a button, the cooker is up and running. Achieves pressure, begins and commencement clock and automatically switches to keep warm once done and left unattended to keep your nourishment warm until the point when you have time for it.

6. **Safety:** Today's pressure cookers (Instant Pot) are worked with the client's security on the most fundamental level. It might have been awful and frequently detonated in the prior days when our moms used them, however present-day variations are considerably more secure to use with their implicit layers and wellbeing highlights which can undoubtedly return any peril.

Instant Pot Preset Functions

1. **Soup button:** The Instant Pot Soup button is pre-set to cook your suppers at high pressure for a default time of 30 minutes. Select the Soup button and the Adjust button once (more) to cook for 40 minutes. Select the Soup button and the Adjust button twice (less) to cook for 20 minutes.

2. **Meat/Stew button:** The Instant Pot Meat/Stew button cooks at High Pressure for a default time of 35 minutes. Changing will give 45 minutes' cook time; Whilst acclimating to less will give you 20 minutes' cook time on High Pressure.

3. **Bean/Chili button:** The Instant Pot Beans/Chili button cooks at High Pressure for a default time of 30 minutes. Contingent upon your coveted cook time, you can select the change button to cook at either 40 minutes or 25 minutes.

4. **Poultry button:** The Instant Pot Poultry button cooks at High Pressure for a default time of 15 minutes. Altering with the modify button will give 30 minutes or 5 minutes cook time contingent upon what you need.

5. **Rice button:** The Instant Pot Rice button cooks on Low Pressure for a default time of 10 minutes. The Rice button is completely automated pre-set button on the Instant Pot. In spite of the fact that the general cook time is highly reliant on the measure of water and rice in the Instant Pot.

6. **Multigrain button:** The Instant Pot Multigrain button cooks at High Pressure for 40 minutes. Changed in accordance with less to get 20 minutes' cook time. Changed in accordance with additional for 45 minutes' warm water dousing time and 1-hour pressure cooking time.

7. **Porridge button:** The Instant Pot Porridge button is pre-set to cook your supper at High Pressure for 20 minutes. Changing will give you 30 moment or 15 minutes' cook time depending. Do not use the quick pressure release method for porridge or other sticky foods. Else, it will make the nourishment squirt out through the vents.

8. **Steam button:** The Instant Pot Steam button cooks at High Pressure for a default time of 10 minutes. Changing in accordance with more will give you 15-minutes cook time. While changing in accordance with less will give you 3-minutes cook time. Use this capacity with a rack or steamer basket since it heats at full power ceaselessly and you don't need your nourishment in coordinate contact with the bottom of the pressure cooking pot.

9. **Slow Cook button:** The Instant Pot Slow Cook button cooks for a default time of 4 hours. Relying upon your coveted cook time, you can press the "+" and "- " button to change to the time given in your formula.

10. **Yogurt button:** The Instant Pot Yogurt button is used for making yogurt in the Instant Pot or individual jugs. It's a one of a kind capacity and another motivation behind why the vast majority pick the Instant Pot pressure cooker over other electric cooker brands.

11. **Manual Function:** The Instant Pot Manual function button is used for Pressure Cooking set up of the pre-set buttons. You can use the if a formula says you should pressure cook at High Pressure for a particular number of minutes. The "+" and "- " buttons can be used to increment or abatement the cooking time.

12. **Timer button:** The Instant Pot Timer button permits to set and leave the Instant Pot to do the cooking at a stipulated time. It can also be used to postpone cooking for up to 24 hours. To use, add whatever you need to be cooked when you're away, into the Instant Pot, push a capacity button (manual, soup, meat and so forth) after which you set the favored cook time took after by the clock button and change in accordance with the quantity of minutes/hours you need cooking to be deferred using the "+" and "- " buttons.

13. **Keep Warm/Cancel button:** The Instant Pot keep warm/ Cancel button is used to keep your nourishment warm in the wake of cooking is improved the situation as long as you need it or until prepared to serve (most extreme of 10 hours). It's generally alright to leave this capacity ON. Unless generally coordinated by a formula you're making.

Instant Pot Parts

The essential parts of this great kitchen apparatus are the inward pot/container and the Lid which empowers the locking, fixing and working up of pressure inside the Instant Pot. And accompanies a locking gadget button that thwarts the cooker from opening while it is under pressure.

The cooker includes some security gadgets on the Lid to control abundance pressure or temperatures and a pressure indicator stick to distinguish the nearness or nonappearance of pressure.

Cooker Lid: The Cooker Lid is the upper piece of the Instant Pot used for fixing the cooker opening when cooking. To open/evacuate it in the wake of cooking, you should first release the pressure from pot using the (QPR) method or using the (NPR) method.

Pressure Indicator: The pressure indicator, is situated on the cooker Lid. It's a little stick situated comfortable top and would ordinarily go up at High Pressure. A similar bind would drop when the pressure point is extremely low showing that it's sheltered to open the cooker. The stick likewise bolts the cooker once in a while, so you can't open the pot when pressure is developed in the Instant Pot.

Steam Release Valve This is the valve used for releasing pressure from the Instant pot (QPR). Or then again when time to add more fixing to pot/check nourishment for doneness. It's the handle situated on the Lid and can be used essentially by swinging to either closing or venting.

Steam Condensation Collector: The Steam Condensation Collector is a holder normally made of plastic which is situated in favor of the cooker. It helps to gather additional build-up.

Silicone Sealing Ring: This is referred to and alluded to as the gasket in a few manuals. And is a fixing ring inside the Lid of the cooker which keeps the steam inside. For security purposes, think about cleaning it subsequent to cooking.

Trivet and Steam Basket: Some Electric Pressure Cooker has a trivet alongside a steam basket. This trivet and the steam basket help to keep the food over the Pressure Cookers bottom. Individuals use the trivet to bubble eggs or steaming their vegetables to keep the supplement from draining into the fluid.

Instant Pot Must-Have Tools (Accessories)

The Instant Pot comes along with lots of accessories. You might need to buy more accessories to get the most out of your meals:

1. **Silicone Egg Mold:** The silicon egg mold can fit in the 5,6,8-quart Pressure Cookers. It is also used for storing smaller portions of dishes and includes a sealing lid.

2. **Silicone Mini Mitts:** The cooking pot usually gets hot when cooking, the mini mitts set can be used to protect your hands when lifting items out of your Pressure Cooker.

3. **Silicone Vegetable Steamer and Lifter:** The steamer / lifter keeps your veggies off the heated bottom of the Instant Pot. The steamer handles are also used to lift items easily from your Pressure Cooker. It can be used to lift a whole chicken out of your Instant Pot without the chicken falling apart.

4. **7-inch Spring Form Non-Stick Pan:** It can be used for baking. It can be used for baking cakes, cheesecakes, and bread. These sizes will fit into your pressure cooker 5,6,8 quarts.

5. **Cook's Stainless-Steel Steamer Basket/Colander:** These tool helps to keep your food items off the bottom of the Instant Pot and out of the water. Food items such as pasta do not require draining when cooking in a Pressure Cooker but having the pasta in this basket helps to easily lift the pasta from the Pressure Cooker.

6. **Clear Lid:** The clear lid comes with a steam vent and handle. It can be used for Sautéing or Slow-Cooking. The clear Lid comes in different sizes such as 3, 6, and 8-quart sizes.

7. **Extra Silicone Rings:** The extra silicone rings are needed on hand at all times. It can be used to switch out rings depending on whether you're cooking a sweet or savory dish.

8. **Steaming Rack:** The steaming rack can be used to steam your veggies, pot-stickers and proteins in your Pressure Cooker.

9. **Mesh steaming basket:** The mesh steaming basket can be used for steaming, frying and straining in the Pressure Cooker. It can also be used for multiple purposes.

10. **Extra Stainless Steel:** It makes it easier to prepare multiple dishes. You just have to switch out the pots rather than cleaning one over and over again.

11. **Cheesecake pan:** The cheesecake pan can be used for making cheesecake in the Pressure Cooker. The bottom is removable but doesn't leak and can be used for dessert after steaming all the veggies.

12. **Instant Read Digital Meat Thermometer:** It can be used for measuring the heat content in the meat while pressure cooking. Having the Meat Thermometer on hand puts an end to serving undercooked or over cooked meat.

Instant Pot FAQ – Frequently Asked Questions

Before Purchasing Instant Pot:
The answers to Frequently Asked Questions before purchasing an Instant Pot are listed below:

1. What is an Instant Pot? Is it the same as a pressure cooker?

YES, the Instant Pot is the same as the Pressure Cooker, it is currently one of the most popular Electric Pressure Cooker models. It is a multi-functional cooker and has some extra functions such as the Rice cooker, Soup, Poultry, Meat, Yogurt, Sauté pan etc.

2. Does the Instant Pot really speed up the cooking process?

Pressure Cooking is faster and saves time and energy. The fast cooking process of the Pressure Cooker may not be noticeable for some foods like broccoli or shrimps. Foods such as pulled pork can be cooked in less than 90 minutes, while it usually takes about 2 to 3 hours to make in the oven.

3. Are there any disadvantages with cooking in the Instant Pot?

YES, the disadvantage of pressure cooking with Pressure Cookers is that you can't inspect, taste, or adjust the food along the way the cooking cycle. That's why it's good to follow the exact recipes instructions with accurate cooking times.

4. Is Instant Pot safe to use?

YES, it's safe to use most modern Electric Pressure Cookers like the Instant Pot are very safe and easy to use. The Instant Pot has about 10 different safety mechanisms to avoid some of the potential issues. It has lots of safety features to prevent potential issues.

5. Can Instant Pot be used for Pressure Canning?

NO, the Instant Pot has not been tested for food safety in pressure canning. The cooking features in Instant Pot IP-CSG, IP-LUX and IP-DUO series are regulated by a pressure sensor instead of a thermometer. Hence, the elevation of your location can disrupt the actual cooking temperature.

6. Can I use the Instant Pot for Pressure Frying?

NO, we would not recommend Pressure Frying in any Electric Pressure Cookers. The Pressure Cooker gasket will melt by the splattering of hot frying oil.

7. What kind of accessories or containers can I use in the Instant Pot?

Any oven-safe accessories and containers can be used in the Instant Pot. Always have in mind that different materials will conduct heat differently and this will make the cooking times to vary. Use stainless steel containers as because they easily conduct heat.

8. I just got my Instant Pot. What should I do first?

Congratulations and welcome aboard! Conduct an initial test run before cooking with the Instant Pot.

9. How to do a Quick Pressure Release (QPR)?

When the timer beeps, carefully move the venting knob from sealing position to venting position. It usually takes a few minutes and rapidly releases the pressure in the Pressure Cooker. Exercise some patient and wait until the floating valve completely, then remove the Lid.

10. How to do a Natural Release (NPR)?

When the timer beeps, you have to exercise patient until the floating valve completely drops before removing the Lid. Carefully turn the venting knob from sealing position to venting position. It will enable all the pressure to release before removing the Lid. (NPR) usually takes about 10 to 25 minutes.

Troubleshooting Tips

Here is a list of instructions to carry out when troubleshooting the Pressure Cooker:

1. Rice is half cooked or too hard:

Possible Reason: The rice contained too little water in the pressure cooker.
Solution: Make sure that the dry rice and water ratio is adjusted according to recipe instructions.
Possible Reason: The Instant Pot lid is removed too early.
Solution: When the timer beeps, leave the Lid on for additional 5 minutes before opening.

2. Rice is too soft:

Possible Reason: The rice contained too much water in the Pressure Cooker.
Solution: Make sure that the dry rice and water ratio is adjusted according to recipe instructions.

3. Difficulty with opening lid:

Possible Reason: This is as a result of pressure inside the Pressure Cooker.
Solution: When the timer beeps, position the steam release handle to the venting position to release the internal pressure. Carefully remove the lid after the pressure is completely released.
Possible Reason: The float valve may be stuck at the popped-up position and causes difficulties in opening the Lid.
Solution: Carefully press the float valve with a pen or long utensil to properly open the Lid.

4. Float valve unable to rise:

Possible Reason: This may result when there is too little food or water in inner pot.
Solution: Pour water according to the recipe instructions.
Possible Reason: This can be caused when the float valve is blocked by the lid locking pin.
Solution: Carefully close the lid completely to prevent the steam from coming out from the steam valve.
Possible Reason: The Steam release valve may not be placed in sealing position.
Solution: Move the steam release handle to the sealing position to seal.

5. Steam leaks from the side of the lid:

Possible Reason: There is no sealing ring in place.
Solution: Carefully install the sealing ring in place.
Possible Reason: The sealing ring might also be destroyed or damaged.
Solution: Replace the destroyed sealing ring with a new one.
Possible Reason: There might be some particles of food debris attached to the sealing ring of the pressure cooker.
Solution: Clean the sealing ring to remove any attached food debris.

6. Steam leaks from float valve for over 2 minutes:

Possible Reason: Some particles of food debris may be attached on the float valve.
Solution: Clean the float valve silicone seal to dislodge any attached food debris.
Possible Reason: The float valve silicone ring may be worn- out and needs to be replaced.
Solution: Replace the worn-out float valve silicone ring with a new one.

CHAPTER 2: BREAKFAST RECIPES

Chocolate Steel Cut Oats

Preparation time: 6 minutes
Cooking time: 9 minutes
Overall time: 15 minutes
Yield: 3-4 people

Recipe Ingredients:
- 1 cup of / 176g / 6.2 oz. of steel cut oats
- 3 medium bananas, (don't use large bananas)
- 3 tablespoons of cocoa
- 3½ cups / 840 mls / 28 fl. oz. of water, or use half non-dairy milk, half water.

Cooking Instructions:
1. Add in the oats, water and cocoa to the Instant Pot and stir.

2. Mash the bananas with a fork until a puree, few small chunks are ok. Add them on top of the other ingredients. (remember, do not stir)

3. Secure the Lid in place and make sure the vent is closed. Select Manual function, set to cook at High Pressure for 9 minutes.

4. When the timer beeps, allow the cooker to release pressure naturally. Remove the Lid carefully and stir the oatmeal before serving. (It will thicken up as it cools).

5. Add more water or milk before serving for a looser texture if you desire.

6. Serve immediately and enjoy!

Cheddar Bacon Ale Dip

Overall time: 25 minutes
Preparation time: 15 minutes
Cooking time: 10 minutes
Makes: 4 to 5 cups

Recipe Ingredients:

- 18 oz. cream cheese, softened
- ¼ cup of sour cream
- 1-1/2 tbsp. Dijon mustard
- 1 teaspoon of garlic powder
- 1 cup of beer or nonalcoholic beer
- 1 lb. of bacon strips, cooked and crumbled
- 2 cups of shredded cheddar cheese
- Heavy whipping cream (¼ cup)
- 1 green onion, thinly sliced
- Soft pretzel bites

Cooking Instructions:

1. Combine cream cheese, sour cream, mustard and garlic powder until smooth in your electric pressure cooker.

2. Then stir in beer, add bacon, reserving 2 tablespoons. Secure the Lid in place and make sure vent is closed.

3. Select the Manual function, set to cook at High Pressure for about 5 minutes.

4. When the time is up, do a quick pressure release. Select the Sauté function and adjust for normal heat.

5. Stir in cheese and heavy cream. Cook and stir until mixture has thickened for about 3 to 4 minutes.

6. Transfer to serving dish. Sprinkle with onion and reserved bacon. Serve with pretzel bun bites.

7. Serve and enjoy.

Scalloped Potatoes

Preparation time: 25 minutes
Cooking time: 15 minutes
Overall time: 40 minutes
Yield: 5-6 people

Cooking Items:

- 7 to 8 small potatoes (2lbs), (peeled and sliced ¼ in thickness)
- 1 cup of vegetable broth
- 3 tbsp. of heavy cream
- ½ teaspoon of salt
- 8 oz. shredded sharp white cheddar (2 oz. reserved for top)
- ¼ tsp. of pepper
- ½ teaspoon of garlic powder
- ½ teaspoon of dried thyme

Cooking Directions:

1. In your Instant Pot, Place sliced potatoes with 1 cup of vegetable broth.

2. Select Manual function, set to cook at High Pressure for 1 minute.

3. When the timer beeps, do a quick pressure release. Preheat your oven on Broil.

4. Transfer the potatoes from the Instant Pot to a pie plate leaving any cooking liquids in your Instant Pot.

5. Add the remaining cooking items (reserving 2 oz. of cheese) to your Instant Pot.

6. Switch your Instant Pot to Sauté mode and stir until smooth. Pour the cheese sauce over the potatoes in the dish and toss to distribute the cheese sauce.

7. Top with reserved cheese. Broil in the oven for 4 to 6 minutes until the top of the potatoes are bubbly and browned.

8. Serve immediately and enjoy.

Egg Muffins with Parmesan, Spinach, and Tomatoes

Preparation time: 15 minutes
Cooking time: 12 minutes
Total time: 27 minutes
Serves: 5-6 people

Recipe Ingredients:
- Non-stick cooking spray
- 8 large eggs
- ¼ cup of (60 ml milk) (We used unsweetened almond milk)
- ¼ tsp. of salt
- 1/8 tsp. of fresh ground black pepper
- 1 cup of (30 g) fresh baby spinach, chopped
- ½ cup of (90 g) diced seeded tomato
- 2 scallions white and green parts, sliced
- 1/3 cup (26.6g) shredded Parmesan cheese (I used Pecorino Romano)

Cooking Directions:
1. Spray 6 (6-oz, or 170 g) ovenproof custard cups with non-stick cooking spray.

2. In a large bowl, whisk together the eggs, milk, salt, and pepper until just blended.

3. Divide the spinach, tomato, and scallions among the custard cups. Then pour the egg mixture over the veggies.

4. Sprinkle the Parmesan over each. Pour in 1 cup (235 ml) water into your pressure cooker and place a steamer rack in the bottom.

5. Place 3 custard cups on the steamer rack and place a second steamer rack on top.

6. Place the remaining 3 cups on it. Secure the Lid, and Select the Manual function, set to cook at High Pressure for about 6 minutes.

7. When the timer beeps, allow the pressure cooker to release pressure naturally for about 5 minutes.

8. Then do a quick pressure release to release the remaining pressure.

9. Remove the Lid carefully and remove the cups. Serve immediately and enjoy.

Banana Oatmeal

Preparation time: 5 minutes
Cooking time: 20 minutes
Overall time: 25 minutes
Serves: 2-3 people

Cooking Items:
- 1 cup of water
- 1 cup of milk [use milk of your choice, we used 1% fat milk]
- ½ cup of steel cut oats
- ¼ tsp. of cinnamon powder
- ½ of a large banana, mashed
- 1 to 2 tablespoons of brown sugar, adjust to taste
- splash of vanilla extract

Toppings:
- peanut butter
- sliced bananas
- almonds/pecans

Cooking Directions:
1. In your Instant Pot, spray the steel pot with a non-stick spray. Add the following accordingly - water, milk, steel cut oats, and cinnamon powder.

2. Add the mashed banana on top (please do not stir). Secure the Lid in place and make sure vent is closed.

3. Select the Porridge button, set to cook for 15 minutes. When the timer beeps, do a quick pressure release.

4. Remove the Lid carefully and stir. Add in brown sugar (or sweetener of choice) and mix everything until well combined.

5. Add a splash of vanilla extract and mix if desired. Serve topped with any topping of choice.

6. Serve immediately and enjoy.

Crustless Crab Quiche

Preparation time: 10 minutes
Cooking time: 50 minutes
Overall time: 1 hour
Yield: 3-4 people

Cooking Items:
- 4 large eggs
- 1 cup half and half
- ½ to 1 teaspoon of salt
- 1 tsp. of pepper
- 1 tsp. of sweet smoked paprika
- 1 tsp. Simply Organic Herbes de Provence, 1 Oz Herbes de Provence
- 1 cup of shredded parmesan or swiss cheese
- 1 cup of chopped green onions green and white parts
- 8 oz. imitation crab meat about 2 cups Or 8 oz. real crab meat, or a mix of crab and chopped raw shrimp

Cooking Directions:
1. Beat together eggs and half and half with a whisk in a medium bowl.

2. Add in salt, pepper, sweet smoked paprika, Herbes de Provence, and shredded cheese. Stir everything with a fork to mix.

3. Add the chopped green onions. After adding the onions, now add in Either the imitation crab meat, real crab meat or some combination of crab meat and chopped raw shrimp.

4. Lay out a sheet of aluminium foil that is cut bigger than the pan you intend to use.

5. Place the spring form pan on this sheet, crimp the sheet about the bottom. You are doing this as most spring form pans can leak a little with liquids.

6. The aluminium foil helps to reduce the mess a little. Pour in the egg mixture into your spring form pan.

7. Cover loosely with foil, then place 2 cups of water into the inner pot of the Instant Pot.

8. Place a steamer rack in the pot, and place the covered spring form pan on the steamer rack.

9. Select Manual button, set to cook at High Pressure for 40 minutes. When the timer beeps.

10. Allow the cooker to release pressure naturally for 10 minutes before doing a quick pressure release.

11. Take out the hot silicone pan. Using a knife, loosen the edges of the quiche from the pan. Remove the outer ring, and serve your delicious crab quiche.

12. Serve and enjoy.

Hard Boiled Eggs

Preparation time: 10 minutes
Cooking time: 5 minutes
Overall time: 15 minutes

Cooking Items:
- Large eggs (as many as you like)
- 1 cup of water

Cooking Directions:
1. Add 1 cup of water into your pot, and place the eggs in a steamer basket.

2. Close and lock the Lid in place, make sure vent is closed. select Manual button, set timer to cook at High Pressure for 5 minutes.

3. When the timer beeps, allow the cooker to release pressure naturally for 5, then do a quick pressure release.

4. Place the hot eggs into cool water to halt the cooking process. You can peel immediately.

5. Serve immediately and enjoy.

Chai Spiced Rice Pudding

Preparation time: 5 minutes
Cooking time: 15 minutes
Overall time: 20 minutes
Yield: 3-4 people
Cooking Items:
- 1 cup of short grain rice, also sold as pudding rice
- 1 cup of almond milk, unsweetened
- 1 cup of coconut milk, unsweetened
- 1½ cups of water
- 2 tbsp. of brown sugar
- 6 Medjool dates, sliced
- 1 tsp. of cinnamon powder
- 1 tsp. of ground ginger powder
- ¼ tsp. of ground nutmeg
- 5 cardamom pods
- (optional) 2 cloves or ¼ teaspoon Allspice powder
- 1 tsp. of vanilla extract
- Pinch of salt

To garnish: berries, nuts, chopped dates or other dried fruit, pistachios, coconut flakes, pineapple, and sliced bananas.
Cooking Directions:
1. Combine all the cooking items, except for the garnishes, in the inner pot. Secure the Lid in place and make sure vent is closed.

2. Select Manual function, set to cook at High Pressure for 10 minutes. When the timer beeps.

3. Allow the cooker to release pressure naturally for 5 minutes. Then do a quick pressure release.

4. Remove the Lid carefully and stir through the rice. Add more water or almond milk, if you like a slightly thinner consistency.

5. Serve topped with your favorite nuts, seeds and dried fruit.

6. Serve immediately and enjoy.

Carrot Cake Oatmeal

Overall time: 20 minutes
Preparation time: 10 min
Cooking time: 10 minutes
Yield: 6-7 people

Recipe Ingredients:

- 4-1/2 cups of water
- 1 can (20 oz.) crushed pineapple, undrained
- 2 cups of shredded carrots
- 1 cup of steel-cut oats
- 1 cup of raisins
- 2 tsp. of ground cinnamon
- 1 tsp. of pumpkin pie spice
- Brown sugar, optional

Cooking Instructions:

1. In your Pressure Cooker coated with cooking spray, combine the first seven ingredients.

2. Secure the Lid in place and make sure vent is closed. Select the Manual function, set timer to cook at High Pressure for about 10 minutes.

3. When the time is up, allow the cooker to release pressure naturally for about 10 minutes before doing a quick pressure release.

4. Sprinkle with brown sugar if you desire.

5. Serve immediately and enjoy.

Baked Apples

Preparation time: 2 minutes
Cooking time: 8 minutes
Overall time: 10 minutes

Cooking Items:

- 6 Apples
- 1 cup of apple juice
- ½ cup of sugar
- 2 tbsp. of cinnamon

Cooking Directions:

1. Firstly, wash and core your apples. Place up to 6 apples in the Instant Pot.

2. Then pour your juice over them. Sprinkle sugar and cinnamon over the apples.

3. Secure the Lid in place and select Manual button, set timer to cook for 8 minutes. When the timer beeps.

4. Do a quick pressure release until float valve drops. Serve hot in bowls with some of your cooking liquid.

5. Serve immediately and enjoy.

Sweet Potato Morning Hash

Preparation time: 10 minutes
Cooking time: 10 minutes
Overall time: 20 minutes
Yield: 3-4 people

Cooking Items:
- 6 large eggs
- 1 tablespoon of Italian seasoning
- ½ tsp. of sea salt
- ½ tsp. of ground black pepper
- ½ lb. of ground pork sausage
- 1 large sweet potato, peeled and cubed
- 1 small onion, peeled and diced
- 2 cloves of garlic, minced
- 1 medium green bell pepper, seeded and diced
- 2 cups water

Cooking Directions:
1. Whisk together the eggs, Italian seasoning, salt, and pepper together in a bowl. Reserve aside.

2. Switch your Instant Pot to Sauté mode, stir-fry sausage, sweet potato, onion, garlic, and bell pepper for 3 to 5 minutes until the onions are translucent.

3. Once onions are translucent, transfer mixture to a 7-cup greased glass dish. Pour whisked eggs over the sausage mixture.

4. Place trivet in the Instant Pot. Then pour in water and place dish with egg mixture onto steamer rack.

5. Secure the Lid in place and make sure vent is closed. Select Manual button, set timer to cook for 5 minutes.

6. When the timer beeps, do a quick pressure release. Remove the Lid carefully and remove dish from Instant Pot.

7. Allow it to sit at room temperature for 5 to 10 minutes to allow the eggs to set.

8. Serve immediately and enjoy!

Breakfast Burrito Casserole

Preparation time: 10 minutes
Cooking time: 13 minutes
Overall time: 23 minutes
Yield: 5-6 people

Cooking Items:
- 4 large eggs
- 2 lb. of red potatoes cubed
- Chopped white or yellow onion (¼ cup)
- 1 diced jalapeno
- 6 oz. ham steak cubed
- ½ tsp. of salt
- ½ teaspoon of mesquite seasoning
- ¼ tsp. of chili powder
- ¾ teaspoon of taco seasoning- instead of mesquite and chili powder use what you have on hand/like.
- **Burrito toppings:** Salsa, avocado, hot sauce and marinated red onions.

Cooking Directions:
1. Mix together the salt, seasonings and eggs and 1 tablespoon of water in a bowl.

2. Beat the egg until the yokes are broken up. Add the onions, potatoes or cheese, ham and jalapeno to the bowl. Add the mixture to the pot you plan to use inside the Instant Pot.

3. Use foil to cover the pot, add 1 cup of water to the Instant Pot. Add the steamer rack to the bottom of the pot.

4. Place the covered pan with the egg mixture on the steamer rack. Make sure the pot is set to sealing.

5. Select Manual button, set timer to cook for 13 minutes. When the time is up, allow it to release pressure naturally.

6. Remove the pan from the instant pot. In a skillet we heated up the tortillas for a few seconds on each side.

7. In each burrito we added a few scoops of the egg mixtures, a slice of avocado, salsa and red onions.

8. Wrap up and enjoy. Serve and enjoy!

Pumpkin Pecan Cake with Maple Cinnamon Sauce

Preparation time: 10 minutes
Cooking time: 30 minutes
Overall time: 40 minutes
Yield: 5-6 people

Cooking Items:
- 8 large eggs
- ¼ cup of brown sugar, lightly packed
- 3 tbsp. of butter, melted
- 1 cup pumpkin
- ½ cup of plain yogurt
- 2 teaspoons of vanilla
- 1½ cups of whole wheat pastry flour
- 1 teaspoon of salt
- 1 tbsp. of baking powder
- 2 tsp. of cinnamon
- 1 ½ tsp. of pumpkin pie spice
- ¾ cup of dried cranberries
- ¾ cup of chopped pecans

Maple Cinnamon Sauce:

- Yogurt (1 cup)
- Maple syrup (¼ cup)
- 1 tsp. of cinnamon
- ½ teaspoon of vanilla extract

Cooking Directions:
1. Grease an 8-inch spring form pan and the heating core (in and out) with non-stick cooking spray. Beat the eggs and sugar together until smooth.

2. Add butter and mix well to combine. Then add pumpkin, yogurt and vanilla. whisk well to combine.

3. Now whisk together the flour, salt, baking powder, cinnamon, and pumpkin spice in a separate bowl.

4. Combine with the egg mixture, fold in the raisins and pecans. Place the heating core in the Centre of the prepared pan.

5. Fill with batter, pour the remaining batter into the pan, ensure to keep the core in the Centre of the pan.

6. Then add in 1 cup of water to the Pressure Cooker pot, place a steamer rack inside.

7. Carefully place the spring form pan on the trivet. Secure the Lid and make sure vent is closed.

8. Select Manual button, set timer to cook at High Pressure for 30 minutes. If not using a Heating Core, set timer to cook at High Pressure for 50 minutes.

9. While the cake is cooking, make the maple cinnamon sauce. Add all of the sauce ingredients into a small bowl, whisk until smooth.

10. When the time is up, allow the Pressure Cooker to release pressure naturally for 10 minutes.

11. Place the pan on a cooling rack and carefully remove the spring form ring. Serve the cake warm with a drizzle of Maple Cinnamon Sauce.

12. Serve immediately and enjoy!

Bread Pudding

Preparation time: 25 minutes
Cooking time 15 minutes
Overall time: 40 minutes
Yield: 8-9 people

Cooking Items:
- 1 loaf of bread grain-free, sourdough, or gluten-free
- 2 cups of milk preferably raw or high-fat coconut
- 4 whole eggs
- ½ cup of pure maple syrup or raw honey, or preferred unrefined sweetener
- ½ cup of butter, melted
- 2 egg yolks
- 1 tbsp. of real vanilla extract
- ¼ teaspoon of sea salt

Cooking Directions:
1. Cut bread into 1" cubes, use bowl that will fit into the Instant Pot stainless steel inner pot.

2. We used a metal bowl with sloping sides that is 4" high and 7-1/2" wide across the top. Place a piece of parchment paper into the bowl, pressing flat any folds.

3. Add cubes to lined bowl, put the following items into blender: eggs, milk, yolks, maple syrup, vanilla and sea salt.

4. Blend for 10 to 15 seconds. With motor still running, add melted butter through the door in Lid.

5. Then add in 2 cups of water to the Instant Pot stainless steel inner pot. Place steamer rack into Instant Pot.

6. Place bowl with bread on top. Now pour custard into bowl, pressing on bread gently so as to wet all the cubes.

7. Place a small square of parchment paper over the surface of the pudding, fold in any corners from the bottom piece that may be sticking out.

8. Secure the Lid in place and make sure vent is closed. Select Steam button, set to cook for 15 minutes.

9. When the timer beeps, allow Pressure Cooker to release pressure naturally for 20 minutes.

10. Select Cancel button, remove the Lid carefully, allow bowl to cool slightly, then remove pudding by lifting up on the corners of parchment that line the bowl.

11. Slice and serve, with optional caramelized pears.

12. Serve and enjoy!

Monkey Bread

Preparation time: 4 minutes
Cooking time 21 minutes
Overall time: 25 minutes
Yield: 2-3 people

Ingredients:

- 1 can of southern buttered grands biscuits
- ½ cup sugar
- 1½ tsp. of cinnamon
- ½ stick of butter
- ½ cup of light brown sugar
- 1 piece of foil.

Cooking Directions:

1. In a medium mixing bowl, add sugar and cinnamon. Mix to combine well.

2. Cut 4 biscuits in quarters, and to sugar mixture, coat thoroughly. Place sugar coated biscuit pieces into a mini loaf pan.

3. Repeat process for the other loaf pan. Add butter and brown sugar in a bowl. Place in the microwave for 45 seconds. Once the butter melts, stir with a fork.

4. Evenly distribute your caramel sauce you made between the two loaf pans. Then add 1 cup of water to the Instant Pot.

5. Place 2 medium sized ramekins in the bottom of the Instant Pot. Place both loaf pans onto ramekins, cover the top of the loaf pans with a piece of foil.

6. Select Manual button, set to cook at High Pressure for 21 minutes. When the timer beeps.

7. Allow the Pressure Cooker to release pressure naturally for 5 minutes before doing a quick pressure release.

8. Serve immediately and enjoy!

CHAPTER 3: POULTRY RECIPES

Salsa Verde Chicken

Preparation time: 5 minutes
Cooking time: 17 minutes
Overall time: 22 minutes
Yield: 8-9 people

Ingredients:

- 3 lb. of boneless, skinless chicken breasts (about 4 chicken breasts)
- 1 (16 oz.) jar Herdez brand salsa Verde (mild)
- Water (½ cup)

Cooking Directions:

1. Put the chicken in your Instant Pot. Pour the salsa verde and water over the top.

2. Secure the Lid and make sure vent is closed. Select Manual button, set timer to cook at High Pressure for 12 minutes (thawed chicken) or 15 minutes (frozen chicken) at High Pressure

3. When the time is up, allow the Pressure Cooker to release pressure naturally for 5 minutes before doing a quick pressure release

4. Remove the Lid carefully, use tongs to move the chicken to a cutting board. Shred the chicken.

5. Stir it back into your Instant Pot. Use chicken in tacos, burritos, quesadillas, over rice, in salad or plain.

6. Serve immediately and enjoy!

Cheesy Chicken and Lentils

Preparation time: 10 minutes
Cooking time: 18 minutes
Overall time: 28 minutes
Yield: 5-6 people

Ingredients:
- 1 cup of dry green lentils
- 1¾ cups of chicken broth
- 1½ lbs. of boneless, skinless chicken breasts or thighs
- 1 teaspoon of cumin
- kosher salt (¼ tsp.)
- ½ teaspoon of garlic powder
- ½ teaspoon of chili powder
- 1 (16 oz.) jar salsa Verde (We used mild)
- 1 (14.5 oz.) can black beans, rinsed and drained
- 1 cup of grated cheddar cheese
- Tortilla chips, cilantro and sour cream, for serving

Ingredients:
1. In your Instant Pot, add in lentils, broth, chicken, cumin, salt, garlic powder, chili powder, salsa verde and beans.

2. Secure the Lid in place and make sure vent is closed. Select Manual button, set to cook for 13 minutes.

3. When the time is up, allow the Pressure cooker to release pressure naturally for 5 minutes before doing a quick pressure release.

4. Use tongs to place chicken on a cutting board. Shred the chicken, stir it back into your Instant Pot.

5. Stir in cheese into the Instant Pot. Serve lentils and chicken plain, in tortillas, as a dip with tortilla chips.

6. Top with tortilla chips, cilantro and sour cream.

7. Serve immediately and enjoy!

Chicken Thighs in Wine Sauce

Overall time: 35 minutes
Preparation time: 15 minutes
Cooking time: 20 minutes
Serves: 3-4 people

Recipe Ingredients:
- 2 tbsp. of butter, divided
- 1 cup of sliced fresh mushrooms
- bone-in chicken thighs, skin removed (about 2¼ lbs.)
- ¼ tsp. of salt
- ¼ tsp. of pepper
- ¼ tsp. of Italian seasoning
- ¼ tsp. of paprika
- 1/3 cup all-purpose flour
- ½ cup of chicken broth
- ½ cup of white wine or additional chicken broth
- 3 green onions, thinly sliced

Cooking Instructions:
1. Select the Sauté function on your Instant Pot, adjust for medium heat your Pressure Cooker.

2. Heat 1 tbsp. of butter. Add mushrooms and cook until tender, for about 3 to 4 minutes.

3. Then remove it and sprinkle chicken with salt, pepper, Italian seasoning and paprika.

4. Place the flour in a shallow bowl. Add chicken, a few pieces at a time, and toss to coat, shake off excess.

5. Heat the remaining butter in your Pressure Cooker, brown both sides of the chicken. Remove.

6. Add broth and wine to cooker, and increase heat to medium-high. Cook for about 2 to 3 minutes, stirring to loosen browned bits from pan.

7. Return the chicken and mushrooms to cooker, then add green onions. Secure the Lid and ensure that the valve is on sealing position.

8. Select the manual function, set to cook at High Pressure for about 10 minutes.

9. When the time is up, allow the Pressure Cooker to release pressure naturally for about 10 minutes, then do a quick pressure release. Serve and enjoy!

Chicken Asparagus Potato Dinner

Preparation time: 16 minutes
Cooking time: 4 minutes
Overall time: 20 minutes
Yield: 5-6 people

Recipe Ingredients:

- 1½ lbs. of (6 small) russet potatoes
- 1½ lb. of boneless, skinless chicken thighs
- 1½ tsp. of salt
- ¾ teaspoon of pepper
- 1½ teaspoons of smoked paprika
- 1½ teaspoons of garlic powder
- Onion powder (1½ tsp.)
- Dried oregano (¾ tsp.)
- Chili powder (1½ tsp.)
- ¾ cup of chicken broth
- 1 bunch of asparagus (washed and cut into 1-inch pieces)

Cooking Directions:

1. Wash the potatoes and peel them. Cut them into 1-inch cubes. Add them into the Instant Pot. Make use of kitchen shears to trim the excess fat off the chicken thighs.

2. Cut the chicken into 1-inch chunks. Add in the cut chicken into your Instant Pot.

3. Add the following ingredients accordingly: salt, pepper, smoked paprika, garlic powder, onion powder, oregano and chili powder.

4. Use a spoon to toss the seasonings to coat the chicken and potatoes. Then, pour the broth into the bottom of your Instant Pot.

5. Secure the Lid in place and make sure the vent is closed. Select Manual button, set to cook at High Pressure for 4 minutes.

6. After the 4 minutes, do a quick pressure release until the float valve drops. Remove the Lid carefully.

7. Stir in the pieces of asparagus and Secure the Lid in place. Allow the pot sit for 5 minutes to warm the asparagus through.

8. Open the Lid, taste and season with salt and pepper if needed. Scoop the chicken, potatoes and asparagus onto plates.

9. Serve immediately and enjoy!

Chicken Soup

Yield: 5-6

Ingredients:
- 2.5 lb. of (1166g) bone-in chicken thighs
- 2 tablespoons (28g) of unsalted butter or olive oil
- 2 (270g) carrots (peeled and chopped)
- 1 (160g) onion, diced
- 5 (18g) of garlic cloves (crushed and minced)
- 1 rib (87g) celery, chopped
- 2 (0.3g) bay leaves
- 4 cups of (1L) unsalted chicken stock
- 4 to 5 (1lb or 454g) Roma tomatoes (quartered)
- 2 tbsp. of (30g) tomato paste
- 2 pinches of dried basil

Cooking Directions:
1. Switch your Instant Pot to Sauté mode, heat up your Instant Pot. Wait until it says Hot (~8 minutes).

2. Pat dry chicken with paper towel, then season one side gently with salt and black pepper.

3. Add in 2 tablespoons of (28g) unsalted butter or olive oil, then quickly add in the chicken (seasoned side) to prevent the butter from burning.

4. Season the other side of chicken with more salt and pepper. Brown both sides of chicken thighs in Instant Pot for about4 minutes per side.

5. Switch Instant Pot to Sauté mode, Sauté onions and garlic, Keep the browned chicken aside.

6. Add in the diced onion in your Instant Pot. And Sauté until soften for about 1 to 2 minutes.

7. Add in 2 tbsp. of (30ml) tomato paste and Sauté for another 1 minute. Add in minced garlic, 2 pinches of dried basil, and 2 bay leaves.

8. Sauté for another 1 minute. Pour in ½ cup of (125ml) unsalted chicken stock.

9. Scrub all the brown bits off the bottom with a wooden spoon. Keep the brown bits as they are very flavorful.

10. Add in browned chicken, chopped celery, chopped carrot, quartered tomatoes, and 3½ cups of (875ml) unsalted chicken stock.

11. Mix well and select Manual button, set to cook at High Pressure for 5 minutes.

12. When the timer beeps, allow the Pressure Cooker to release pressure naturally for 15 minutes.

13. Place pressure cooked chicken in a large bowl, shred the chicken with two forks.

14. Discard the bones and skins. Add back shredded chicken in the Instant Pot. Taste the soup and season with more salt if necessary.

15. Serve immediately and enjoy!

Hearty Chicken & Potatoes

Preparation time: 15 minutes
Cooking time: 20 minutes
Overall time: 35 minutes
Serves: 3 to 4 people

Recipe Ingredients:

- 1 large leek (white and pale green parts only), halved, washed and diced
- 1 oz. / 28 g of butter (salted or unsalted)
- 2 medium chicken breasts (0.7 lb. / 350 g), diced
- 4 skinless chicken thighs (0.5 lb. / 300g), diced
- 3 to 4 large potatoes (about 1.7 lb. / 800 g), diced into large cubes (larger than chicken pieces)
- 1 large carrot, sliced
- 3 cloves of garlic, chopped
- (optional) ½ cup of frozen peas
- 2 bay leaves
- 1 cube of chicken stock (or 400 ml / 1.5 cups broth)
- Zest of ½ lemon
- 2 tbsp. of lemon juice
- 1½ teaspoon of salt
- ½ tsp. of white or black pepper
- 400 ml (1½ cups) of water

Cooking Directions:

1. Switch your Instant Pot to Sauté mode, add the leeks and butter. Cook until softened for about 4 to 5 minutes.

2. Add the rest of the ingredients. Reserve half of the peas (if using) for later. Give everything a good stir.

3. Select Keep Warm/Cancel button, to stop the Sauté process. Secure the Lid and make sure vent is closed.

4. Select Manual button, set to cook at High Pressure for 10 minutes. After 10 minutes, allow the cooker to release pressure naturally for about 10 minutes.

5. Add the remaining frozen peas to a bowl of boiling hot water to defrost. Remove the Lid, stir through.

6. Serve topped with the remaining defrosted peas and a little extra lemon zest and black pepper for garnish, if you desire.

7. Serve and enjoy!

Whole Chicken

Preparation time: 5 minutes
Cooking time: 45 minutes
Overall time: 50 minutes
Yield: 5 to 6 people

Ingredients:
- 1 whole chicken (completely thawed if frozen)
- ½ stick softened butter
- 1 teaspoon of salt
- ½ tsp. of pepper
- Smoked paprika (½ tsp.)
- Onion powder (½ tsp.)
- Garlic powder (½ tsp.)
- ¼ tsp. of dried oregano
- 1 cup of water
- 1 Lemon, cut in half

Cooking Directions:
1. Remove the chicken from the packaging and place it on a plastic cutting board. Pat dry with paper towels. Add butter and seasonings in a mixing bowl.

2. Mix with a fork and rub the compound butter all over the chicken.

3. Add water into your Instant Pot liner, followed by the steamer rack that came with the Instant Pot.

4. Place the whole chicken on top of the steamer rack. Secure the Lid in place and make sure vent is closed.

5. Select Manual button, set to cook at High Pressure for 45 minutes. After the 45 minutes.

6. Allow the Pressure Cooker to release pressure naturally for 15 minutes before doing a quick pressure release.

7. Remove carefully from the pot onto a platter. Finish with drizzle of the leftover cooking liquid and a squeeze of lemon juice.

8. Serve immediately and enjoy!

BBQ Whole Chicken

Overall time: 35 minutes
Preparation time: 5 minutes
Cooking time: 30 minutes
Yield: 5-6 people

Ingredients:

- BBQ rub
- 4 lbs. of whole chicken
- Olive oil
- 1/3 cup apple juice

Cooking Directions:

1. Prepare the BBQ rub and massage it both under and over the skin. Drizzle some oil in the Instant Pot.

2. Switch your Instant Pot to Sauté mode and allow it to heat up. Place the whole chicken, breast side down in the Instant Pot.

3. If it is too big to lay down flat, you'll have to brown the skin on the stove top in a large skillet.

4. Cook until golden and turn over, browning the other side. Leave the chicken in the pot.

5. Pour in the liquids, secure the Lid and make sure vent is closed. Select Manual button, set to cook at High Pressure for 30 minutes.

6. After the 30 minutes, allow the Instant Pot to release pressure naturally for 5 minutes before doing a quick pressure release.

7. Serve immediately and enjoy!

Whole Roast Chicken

Preparation time: 10 minutes
Cooking time: 40 minutes
Overall time: 50 minutes
Yield: 1 chicken

Ingredients:

- One small chicken (about 4 lbs.)
- 1 tbsp. of coconut oil
- Salt and pepper to taste
- Additional seasonings if desired

Cooking Directions:

1. Switch your Instant Pot to Sauté mode, and add in the coconut oil. When the oil heats up.

2. Place the chicken in breast-down and brown. When the chicken is brown, turn it over and place it on the steamer rack that comes with the pot.

3. Add in ½ cup of water and sprinkle the chicken with seasoning. Secure the Lid and make sure vent is closed.

4. Select Poultry button, set to cook at High Pressure for 24 minutes. If it's smaller or larger, calculate how much time it should cook by multiplying the number of pounds by 6 minutes.

5. 3 pounds of chicken would be 18 minutes and a 5 pounds of chicken would be 30 minutes.

6. When the timer beeps, allow the Pressure Cooker to release pressure naturally for few minutes.

7. Serve immediately and enjoy!

Chicken Enchilada Soup

Overall time: 45 minutes
Preparation time: 25 minutes
Cooking time: 20 minutes
Serve: 8 (3-¼ qt.)

Ingredients:

- 1 tbsp. of canola oil
- 2 Anaheim pepper or poblano pepper, finely chopped
- 1 medium onion, chopped
- 3 garlic cloves, minced
- 1 lb. of boneless skinless chicken breasts
- 1 carton (48 oz.) of chicken broth
- 1 can (14-1/2 oz.) Mexican diced tomatoes, undrained
- 1 can (10 oz.) enchilada sauce
- 2 tablespoons of tomato paste
- 1 tbsp. of chili powder
- 2 teaspoon of ground cumin
- ½ tsp. of pepper
- (Optional) ½ to 1 tsp. of chipotle hot pepper sauce
- 1/3 cup of minced fresh cilantro
- (Optional): shredded cheddar cheese, cubed avocado, sour cream and tortilla strips

Cooking Directions:

1. Switch your Instant Pot to Sauté mode, adjust for high heat, then add in oil.

2. Add in peppers and onion, cook and stir until tender for 6 to 8 minutes. Add in garlic and cook for 1 minute longer.

3. Add in chicken, broth, tomatoes, enchilada sauce, tomato paste, seasonings and, if desired, pepper sauce.

4. Give everything a good stir. Secure the Lid and ensure that the valve is on sealing Position.

5. Select the Manual function, set to cook at High Pressure for about 8 minutes.

6. When the time is up, allow the cooker to release pressure naturally for about 7 minutes before doing a quick pressure release.

7. Remove chicken from the Pressure Cooker. Shred with two forks; return to pressure cooker.

8. Stir in cilantro. Serve with toppings as desired. Serve and enjoy!

Honey Garlic Chicken

Preparation time: 5 minutes
Cooking time: 20 minutes
Overall time: 25 minutes
Serves: 3-4 people

Recipe Ingredients:
- 1/3 cup of honey
- 4 cloves garlic, minced
- ½ cup of low sodium soy sauce
- ½ cup no salt ketchup
- ½ tsp. of dried oregano
- 2 tbsp. of chopped fresh parsley
- 1 tbsp. of sesame seed oil
- 4 to 6 bone-in, skinless chicken thighs
- salt and fresh ground pepper
- (for garnish) ½ tbsp. of toasted sesame seeds
- (for garnish) sliced green onions

Cooking Instructions:
1. In a mixing bowl, combine honey, minced garlic, soy sauce, ketchup, oregano and parsley, mix until well combined, reserve aside.

2. Switch your Instant Pot to Sauté mode, heat the Instant Pot. Add in sesame oil to the pot.

3. Season the chicken thighs with salt and pepper, then arrange in the Instant Pot. Cook for about 2 to 3 minutes per side.

4. Add the prepared honey garlic sauce to the pot. Secure the Lid and make sure vent is closed.

5. Select the Poultry button, set to cook for 20 minutes. After the 20 minutes, allow the Pressure Cooker to release pressure naturally for 5 minutes.

6. Transfer the chicken to a serving plate and spoon the sauce over the chicken. Garnish with toasted sesame seeds and green onions if you like.

7. Serve immediately and enjoy.

Jamaican Jerk Chicken Thighs

Preparation time: 15 minutes
Cooking time: 20 minutes
Overall time: 35 minutes
Yield: 3-4 people

Ingredients:
- 4 chicken thighs (fat-trimmed)
- 1 habanero, chopped
- 1 tbsp. of reduced-sodium soy sauce
- 1 lime, juice of
- 1/3 cup of pineapple juice
- ½ onion, chopped
- 3 green onions (scallions), chopped
- 1 tsp. of cinnamon
- 1 teaspoon of fresh or jarred ginger
- ½ teaspoon of nutmeg
- 1 tsp. of ground allspice
- 3 garlic cloves, chopped
- 1 tablespoon of olive oil
- 2 teaspoons of creole seasoning, (We used tony chachere)
- Salt and pepper

Cooking Directions:
1. Combine all the recipe ingredients in a blender (except for the olive oil and chicken).

2. Blend well for 30 seconds. Rinse the chicken and pat dry, place the chicken in a Ziploc bag and drizzle ½ of the marinade over the chicken in the bag.

3. Seal the bag tightly and refrigerate for about 2 hours, preferably overnight, to marinate.

4. Add olive oil into your Instant Pot. Switch your Instant Pot to Sauté mode and brown both sides of the chicken for 4 to 5 minutes.

5. Drizzle the remaining marinade over the chicken. Secure the Lid in place and make sure the valve is sealed.

6. Select Manual button, set to cook at High Pressure for 14 minutes. After the 14 minutes, do a quick release until float valve drops.

7. Serve and enjoy!

Chicken Cacciatore

Overall time: 35 minutes
Preparation time: 10 minutes
Cooking time: 25 minutes

Ingredients:

- 4 chicken thighs, with the bone, skin removed
- kosher salt and fresh pepper
- Olive oil spray
- ½ can (14 oz.) crushed tomatoes
- Diced onion (½ cup)
- ¼ cup of diced red bell pepper
- Diced green bell pepper (½ cup)
- Dried oregano (½ tsp.)
- 1 bay leaf
- 2 tbsp. of chopped basil or parsley for topping

Cooking Directions:

1. Firstly, season chicken with salt and pepper on both sides. Then switch your Instant Pot to Sauté mode.

2. Lightly spray with oil and brown chicken on both sides for a few minutes. Reserve aside.

3. Spray with a little more oil and add onions and peppers. Sauté for 5 minutes until soften and golden.

4. Pour tomatoes over the chicken and vegetables. Then add oregano, bay leaf, salt and pepper, give everything a good stir.

5. Secure the Lid in place and make sure vent is closed. Select Manual button, set to cook at High Pressure for 25 minutes.

6. When the timer beeps, allow the cooker to release pressure naturally for few minutes.

7. Remove bay leaf, garnish with parsley and serve over pasta. Serve and enjoy!

Chicken Adobo

Preparation time: 10 minutes
Cooking time: 30 minutes
Overall time: 40 minutes
Serves: 3-4 people

Recipe Ingredients:

- (995g) chicken thighs or 2 lb. of chicken meat
- Green onions, chopped for garnish
- 1 tbsp. of peanut oil or vegetable oil
- 12 (34g) garlic cloves, crushed
- 1 (150g) medium onion, sliced
- 1 tsp. of (4g) whole black peppercorn
- 1 dried red chili
- 4 dried bay leaves

Adobo Sauce:

- ¼ cup of (63ml) Filipino soy sauce
- ⅓ cup of (83ml) light soy sauce (not low sodium soy sauce)
- ⅓ cup of (83ml) Filipino vinegar
- 1 tbsp. (15ml) fish sauce
- 1 tbsp. of (12.5g) sugar

Cornstarch mixture:

- 2.5 tbsp. of (22.5g) cornstarch
- 3 tbsp. of (45ml) cold water

Pot in Pot Rice:

- 1 cup (235g) Jasmine rice, rinsed and drained well
- 1 cup (250ml) cold water

Garnish:

- stalk green onion, thinly sliced

Cooking Directions:

1. Switch the Instant Pot to Sauté mode. adjust button to Sauté More. Wait until indicator says Hot.

2. In a medium glass measuring cup, mix and combine 1 tablespoon of (12.5g) sugar, 1 tbsp. of (15ml) fish sauce, ¼ cup of (63ml) Filipino soy sauce, ⅓ cup (83ml) light soy sauce, and ⅓ cup (83ml) Filipino vinegar.

3. Add in 1 tbsp. of (15ml) oil in Instant Pot. Sauté onions for about 2 minutes. Add 12 crushed garlic cloves, 1 teaspoon of (4g) whole black peppercorn, dried red chili, and 4 dried bay leaves and sauté for another 45 seconds.

4. Add in adobo sauce mixture in the Instant Pot and deglaze the bottom of the pot with a wooden spoon.

5. Coat the chicken with adobo sauce by dipping the skin side into the adobo sauce, then flip to place them skin side up in Instant Pot.

6. Place a steamer rack in the Instant Pot and layer a stainless-steel bowl with 1 cup (235g) Jasmine rice + 1 cup (250ml) cold water on top.

7. Secure the Lid and make sure vent is closed. Select the Manual function, set to cook at High Pressure for about 6 minutes.

8. When the time is up, allow the cooker to release pressure naturally for about 10 minutes before doing a quick pressure release.

9. Remove the Lid carefully. Remove stainless steel bowl & steamer rack. Set aside the chicken thighs in a serving bowl.

10. Select the Cancel button, then select the Sauté button to heat up the sauce. In a small mixing bowl, mix 2.5 tbsp. of (22.5g) cornstarch with 3 tbsp. of (45ml) cold water.

11. Mix it in one third at a time until desired thickness. Taste and season with more vinegar, sugar, or soy sauce accordingly if necessary.

12. Coat chicken thighs with adobo sauce by placing them back in the pot.

13. **Optional Step to Crisp Skin:** Place chicken adobo (coated with a thin layer of sauce on top) on a baking tray and put it under a broiler for about 5 to 10 minutes to maximize the flavor and crisp up the skin.

14. Serve chicken adobo with Jasmine rice. Drizzle lightly with the adobo sauce and garnish with green onions on top.

15. Serve immediately and enjoy.

Pasta Bolognese

Preparation time: 5 minutes
Cooking time: 25 minutes
Overall time: 30 minutes
Serves: 3-4 people

Recipe Ingredients:

- ½ lb. (227 grams) ground beef
- 1 lb. (454g) penne rigate
- 12 white mushrooms, sliced
- 3 cloves garlic, minced
- 1 celery, (chopped)
- 1 small onion, sliced
- A dash of sherry wine
- A pinch of dried oregano
- A pinch of dried basil
- Kosher salt and black pepper
- Olive oil

Pasta Sauce:

- 1 cup of unsalted chicken stock + 2 cups of water
- fl. oz can (156 ml) tomato paste
- 2 tbsp. of light soy sauce (not low sodium soy sauce)
- 1 tbsp. of fish sauce
- 1 tbsp. of Worcestershire sauce

Cooking Instructions:

1. Switch your Instant Pot to Sauté mode and heat up the Pressure Cooker. Select the Meat/Chicken button.

2. Make sure the pot is as hot as it can be before placing any ingredient in the pot. Add in 1 tbsp. of olive oil in the Pressure Cooker.

3. Ensure to coat the oil over the whole bottom of the pot. Add ½ pound of ground beef, season with kosher salt and ground black pepper.

4. Moisture begins to come out of ground beef. Allow the moisture to evaporate.

5. Browning begins due to maillard reaction. Remove & set aside. Sauté the Onion, Garlic, Celery and Mushrooms.

6. Add in 1 tbsp. of olive oil and sliced onion, sauté. Add a pinch of kosher salt and ground black pepper to season.

7. Stir occasionally until slightly browned. Add minced garlic and stir for roughly 30 seconds until fragrant.

8. Add in sliced mushrooms, chopped celery, a pinch of dried oregano, and dried basil. Cook for another minute.

9. Taste and season with kosher salt and ground black pepper if necessary. Pour in a dash of sherry wine and deglaze the bottom of the pot with a wooden spoon.

10. Add browned ground beef, 1 cup of unsalted chicken stock, 2 cups of water, 2 tbsp. of light soy sauce, 1 tbsp. of fish sauce, and 1 tbsp. of Worcestershire sauce. Mix everything together.

11. Pour 450 g of Penne pasta into the sauce. Place 156 ml tomato paste on top of the pasta. Mixing 156 ml tomato paste with 3 cups of liquid should be completely safe.

12. Avoid mixing the tomato paste if you are afraid of scorching. Taste and season with kosher salt and ground black pepper if necessary.

13. Ensure that all the Penne pasta are completely submerged into the sauce.

14. Secure the Lid and make sure vent is closed. Select the Manual function, set to cook at High Pressure for about 4 minutes.

15. When the time is up, allow to release pressure naturally for about 5 minutes before doing a quick pressure release.

16. Give everything a good stir. Taste one of the Penne pasta. If you find the texture too hard, secure the Lid and let the leftover heat cook them until desired doneness.

17. Sprinkle some freshly grated Parmesan cheese to kick it up a notch.

18. Serve immediately and enjoy!

Chicken Shawarma

Preparation time: 10 minutes
Cooking time: 15 minutes
Overall time: 25 minutes

Ingredients:

- 1 to 1.5 lb. of boneless skinless chicken breasts
- 1 to 1.5 lb. of boneless skinless chicken thighs
- 1 tsp. of ground cumin
- 1 tsp. of paprika
- ½ tsp. of turmeric
- ¼ tsp. of granulated garlic
- ¼ tsp. of ground allspice
- ¼ tsp. of chili powder
- 1/8 tsp. of ground cinnamon
- Kosher salt and freshly ground black pepper
- 1 cup of chicken broth

Cooking Instructions:

1. Slice the chicken breasts and thighs into strips and place into your Instant Pot.

2. In a small mixing bowl, combine all of spices (cumin – cinnamon). Now pour the spice mix over the chicken with a pinch of salt and some pepper. Mix it all together so the spices evenly coat the chicken.

3. Then add the chicken broth to your Instant Pot. Secure the Lid in place and make sure vent is closed.

4. Select Poultry button, set to cook for about 15 minutes. After the 15 minutes, allow the Pressure Cooker to release pressure naturally for 10 minutes.

5. Do a quick pressure release until the float valve drops. Remove the Lid carefully.

6. Serve with veggies or on sweet potato toast drizzled with tahini sauce.

7. Serve and enjoy!

CHAPTER 4: MEAT RECIPES

Mesquite Ribs

Overall time: 45 minutes
Preparation time: 10 minutes
Cooking time: 35 minutes
Yield: 7-8 people

Recipe Ingredients:
- 1 cup of water
- 2 tbsp. of cider vinegar
- 1 tbsp. of soy sauce
- 4 lbs. of pork baby back ribs (cut into serving-size portions)
- 2 tbsp. of mesquite seasoning
- ¾ cup of BBQ sauce, divided

Cooking Directions:
1. Combine water, vinegar and soy sauce in the Pressure Cooker. Rub ribs with mesquite seasoning.

2. Add the ribs to the Pressure Cooker. Secure the Lid and make sure vent is closed. Select Manual button, set to cook at High Pressure for about 35 minutes.

3. When the time is up, allow the cooker to release pressure naturally for about 10 minutes before doing a quick pressure release.

4. Remove ribs to a foil-lined baking sheet and preheat broiler. Brush ribs with barbecue sauce.

5. Broil 4 to 6 in. from heat until glazed. Serve with additional barbecue sauce if desired.

6. Serve immediately and enjoy!

Pork Picadillo Lettuce Wraps

Total time: 55 minutes
Prep: 30 minutes
Cooking: 25 minutes
Makes: 2 dozen

Recipe Ingredients:

- 3 garlic cloves, minced
- 1 tbsp. of chili powder
- 1 tsp. of salt
- ½ tsp. of pumpkin pie spice
- ½ tsp. of ground cumin
- ½ tsp. of pepper
- 2 pork tenderloins (1 lb. each)
- 1 large onion, chopped
- 1 small Granny Smith apple (peeled and chopped)
- 1 small sweet red pepper, chopped
- 1 can (10 oz.) diced tomatoes and green chilies, undrained
- 1 cup of water
- ½ cup of golden raisins
- ½ cup of chopped pimiento-stuffed olives
- 24 Bibb or Boston lettuce leaves
- ¼ cup of slivered almonds, toasted

Cooking Instructions:

1. Mix the minced garlic and seasonings, then rub over pork. Transfer to a 6-qt. Pressure Cooker.

2. Add in the onion, apple, sweet pepper, tomatoes and water. Secure the Lid and make sure vent is closed.

3. Select the Manual function, set to cook at High Pressure for about 25 minutes.

4. When the time is up, allow the cooker to release pressure naturally for about 10 minutes before doing a quick pressure release.

5. Remove the pork and allow it to cool, shred meat into bite-size pieces. Then return it back to your Pressure Cooker.

6. Select the Sauté function and adjust for low heat. Stir in raisins and olives; heat through.

7. Serve in lettuce leaves and sprinkle with almonds.

8. Serve and enjoy!

Melt-in-Your-Mouth Chuck Roast

Total time: 55 minutes
Preparation time: 20 minutes
Cooking time: 35 minutes
Serves: 5 to 6 people

Recipe Ingredients:
- 1 can (14-1/2 oz.) Italian stewed tomatoes, undrained
- ½ cup of beef broth
- ½ cup of ketchup
- 3 tbsp. of brown sugar
- 2 tbsp. of Worcestershire sauce
- 4 tsp. of prepared mustard
- 3 garlic cloves, minced
- 1 tbsp. of soy sauce
- 2 tsp. of pepper
- ¼ tsp. of crushed red pepper flakes
- 1 large onion, halved and sliced
- 1 medium green pepper, halved and sliced
- 1 celery rib, chopped
- 1 boneless beef chuck roast (2 to 3 lb.)
- 3 tbsp. of cornstarch
- ¼ cup of cold water

Cooking Instructions:
1. mix first 10 ingredients in medium bowl. Place onion, green pepper and celery in your Pressure Cooker, place roast over top.

2. Pour tomato mixture over roast. Secure the Lid in place and make sure vent is closed.

3. Select the Manual function, set to cook at High Pressure for about 35 minutes.

4. When the time is up, allow the cooker to release pressure naturally for about 10 minutes before doing a quick pressure release.

5. Remove roast. Strain cooking juices, reserving vegetables. Skim fat from juices.

6. Return juices to the Pressure Cooker. Switch your Pressure Cooker to Sauté mode and adjust for high heat, bring juices to a boil.

7. In a small mixing bowl, mix cornstarch and water until smooth, stir into cooking juices.

8. Cook and stir until sauce is thickened, for about 1 to 2 minutes. Return beef mixture to pressure cooker and give everything a good stir.

9. Serve roast and vegetables with gravy.

10. Serve and enjoy!

Beef Carnitas

Overall time: 1 hr. 20 minutes
Preparation time: 40 minutes
Cooking time: 40 minutes
Yield: 16 servings

Recipe Ingredients:
- 2 tbsp. of kosher salt
- 2 tbsp. of packed brown sugar
- 1 tbsp. of ground cumin
- 1 tbsp. of smoked paprika
- 1 tbsp. of chili powder
- 1 tsp. of garlic powder
- 1 tsp. of ground mustard
- 1 tsp. of dried oregano
- 1 tsp. of cayenne pepper
- 3 lb. of boneless beef chuck roast
- 3 tbsp. of canola oil
- 2 large sweet onion, thinly sliced
- 3 poblano pepper, seeded and thinly sliced
- 2 chipotle peppers in adobo sauce (finely chopped)
- 1 jar (16 oz.) salsa
- 16 flour tortillas (8 inches), warmed
- 3 cups of crumbled queso fresco or shredded Monterey Jack cheese

Optional toppings: cubed avocado, sour cream and minced fresh cilantro

Cooking Instructions:
1. Mix the first nine ingredients. Cut roast in half, rub with ¼ cup of spice mixture.

2. Cover remaining mixture and store in a cool dry place. Select the Sauté function on your Pressure Cooker and adjust for high heat, add oil.

3. Brown roast on all sides. Place onions and peppers on meat. Top with salsa.

4. Secure the Lid in place and make sure the steam valve is on sealing position.

5. Select the Manual function, set to cook at High Pressure for about 40 minutes.

6. When the time is up, allow the cooker to release pressure naturally for about 10 minutes before doing a quick pressure release.

7. Remove roast and shred with two forks. Skim fat from cooking juices. Return meat to Pressure Cooker, heat through.

8. Using a slotted spoon, place ½ cup of meat mixture on each tortilla. Sprinkle with cheese.

9. Add toppings of your choice.

10. Serve immediately and enjoy!

Lamb Shanks with Garlic and Port Wine

Overall time: 45minutes
Preparation time: 10 minutes
Cooking time: 30 minutes
Serves: 2-3 people

Recipe Ingredients:

- 2 lb. of lamb shanks
- Salt, to taste
- Pepper, to taste
- 1 tbsp. of olive oil
- 10 garlic cloves, peeled and left whole
- ½ cup of chicken stock (or other broth)
- ½ cup of port wine
- 1 tbsp. of tomato paste
- ½ tsp. of dried rosemary
- 1 tbsp. of unsalted butter
- 1 tsp. of balsamic vinegar (up to 2 tsp.)

Cooking Instructions:

1. Trim excess fat from the lamb shanks and season with salt and pepper.

2. Heat the oil in the Pressure Cooker. Add the shanks and brown on all sides.

3. When the shanks are completely browned, add the garlic cloves and cook until they are lightly browned but not burned.

4. Add the stock, port, tomato paste, and rosemary, stirring so the tomato paste dissolves.

5. Secure the Lid and make sure the vent is closed. Select the Manual function, set to cook at High Pressure for 30 minutes.

6. When the time is up, allow the cooker to release pressure naturally. Remove the lamb shanks.

7. Return pan to heat and boil the liquid, uncovered, for 5 minutes to reduce and thicken the sauce.

8. Whisk in the butter, then add the vinegar. Serve the sauce over the lamb.

9. Serve and enjoy!

Cuban Pulled Pork Sandwiches

Total time: 45 minutes
Preparation time: 20 minutes
Cooking time: 25 minutes
Makes: 16 servings
Recipe Ingredients:
- 1 boneless pork shoulder butt roast (4 to 5 lb.)
- 2 tsp. of salt
- 2 tsp. of pepper
- 1 tbsp. of olive oil
- 1 cup of orange juice
- ½ cup of lime juice
- 12 garlic cloves, minced
- 2 tbsp. of spiced rum, optional
- 2 tbsp. of ground coriander
- 2 tsp. of white pepper
- 1 tsp. of cayenne pepper

Sandwiches:
- 2 loaves (1 lb. each) French bread
- Yellow mustard, optional
- 16 dill pickle slices
- 1½ lb. thinly sliced deli ham
- 1½ lb. Swiss cheese, sliced

Cooking Instructions:
1. Cut the pork into 2-in.-thick pieces and season with salt and pepper.

2. Select the Sauté function on your Pressure Cooker, adjust for high heat. Add oil, working in batches, brown pork on all sides.

3. Remove from cooker. Add orange and lime juices, stirring to scrape browned bits from bottom of the pot.

4. Add in garlic, rum, if desired, coriander, white pepper and cayenne pepper. Return pork and any collected juices to cooker.

5. Secure the Lid and make sure vent is closed. Select the Manual function, set to cook at High Pressure for about 25 minutes.

6. When the time is up, allow the cooker to release pressure naturally for about 10 minutes before doing a quick pressure release.

7. Remove roast, allow it to cool, shred with two forks. Remove 1 cup cooking liquid from cooker; add to pork and toss.

8. Cut each loaf of bread in half lengthwise. If desired, spread mustard over cut sides of bread.

9. Layer bottom halves of bread with pickles, pork, ham and cheese. Replace tops. Cut each loaf into eight slices.

10. Serve and enjoy!

Easy Pork Posole

Total time: 40 minutes
Preparation time: 30 minutes
Cooking time: 10 minutes
Makes: 8 servings

Recipe Ingredients:

- 1 tbsp. of canola oil
- ½ lb. of boneless pork shoulder butt roast, cubed
- ½ lb. of Johnsonville Fully Cooked Andouille Sausage Rope, sliced
- 2 medium tomatoes, seeded and chopped
- 1 can (15 oz.) hominy, rinsed and drained
- 1 cup minced fresh cilantro
- 1 medium onion, chopped
- 4 green onions, chopped
- 1 jalapeno pepper, seeded and chopped
- 2 garlic cloves, minced
- 1 tbsp. of chili powder
- 1 tsp. of ground cumin
- ½ tsp. of cayenne pepper
- ½ tsp. of coarsely ground pepper
- cups of reduced-sodium chicken broth

Optional ingredients: corn tortillas, chopped onion, minced fresh cilantro and lime wedges

Cooking Instructions:

1. Select the Sauté function on your Instant Pot and adjust for normal heat. Add oil. Add pork cubes and sausage.

2. Cook and stir until browned. Remove pork and sausage, drain. Return meats to the Pressure Cooker.

3. Add next 12 ingredients. Secure the Lid in place and make sure vent is closed.

4. Select the Manual function, set to cook at High Pressure for about 10 minutes.

5. When the time is up, allow the cooker to release pressure naturally for 5 minutes before doing a quick pressure release.

6. Serve with tortillas, onion, cilantro and lime wedges if desired.

7. Serve and enjoy!

Beef Tips

Overall time: 35 minutes
Preparation time: 20 minutes
Cooking time: 15 minutes
Serves: 3-4 people

Recipe Ingredients:

- 3 tsp. of olive oil
- 1 beef top sirloin steak (1 lb.), cubed
- ½ tsp. of salt
- ¼ tsp. of pepper
- 1/3 cup of dry red wine or beef broth
- ½ lb. of sliced baby portobello mushrooms
- 1 small onion, halved and sliced
- 2 cups of beef broth
- 1 tbsp. of Worcestershire sauce
- 3 to 4 tbsp. of cornstarch
- ¼ cup of cold water
- Hot cooked mashed potatoes

Cooking Instructions:

1. Select the Sauté function on your Instant Pot and adjust for high heat. Add in 2 tsp. of oil.

2. Sprinkle beef with salt and pepper. Brown meat in batches, adding oil as needed.

3. Transfer the beef to a medium bowl. Add wine to cooker, stirring to loosen browned bits.

4. Return beef to cooker, add mushrooms, onion, broth and Worcestershire sauce.

5. Secure the Lid and make sure vent is closed. Select the Manual function, set to cook at High Pressure for about 15 minutes.

6. When the time is up, do a quick pressure release. Select Sauté function and adjust for high heat, bring liquid to a boil.

7. In a small bowl, mix cornstarch and water until smooth; gradually stir into beef mixture.

8. Cook and stir until sauce is thickened, 1 to 2 minutes. Serve with mashed potatoes. Serve and enjoy!

Beef Brisket in Beer

Overall time: 1 hr. 25 minutes
Preparation time: 15 minutes
Cook: 70 minutes
Serves: 5-6 people

Recipe Ingredients:
- 1 fresh beef brisket (2-1/2 to 3 lb.)
- 2 tsp. of liquid smoke, optional
- 1 tsp. of celery salt
- ½ tsp. of pepper
- ¼ tsp. of salt
- 1 large onion, sliced
- 1 can (12 oz.) beer or nonalcoholic beer
- 2 tsp. of Worcestershire sauce
- 2 tbsp. of cornstarch
- ¼ cup of cold water

Cooking Instructions:
1. Cut brisket in half, rub with liquid smoke if you like, along with celery salt, pepper and salt.

2. Place brisket fatty side up in your Pressure Cooker and top with onion. Combine beer and Worcestershire sauce, pour over meat.

3. Secure the Lid in place and make sure vent is closed. Select the Manual function, set to cook at High Pressure for about 70 minutes.

4. When the time is up, allow the cooker to release pressure naturally for 10 minutes before doing a quick pressure release.

5. If brisket isn't fork-tender, reseal cooker and cook for an additional 10 to 15 minutes at High Pressure.

6. Remove brisket, cover with foil and keep warm. Strain cooking juices, then return juices to the Pressure Cooker.

7. Select the Sauté function and adjust for high heat, bring liquid to a boil. In a small bowl, mix cornstarch and water until smooth.

8. Gradually stir in the cornstarch mixture into juices. Cook and stir until sauce is thickened for about 2 minutes.

9. Serve with beef and enjoy.

Cajun Pork and Rice

Total time: 40 minutes
Preparation time: 20 minutes
Cooking time: 20 minutes
Makes: 4 servings

Recipe Ingredients:
- 1 tsp. of olive oil
- 1 medium green pepper, julienned
- 1½ tsp. of ground cumin
- 1½ tsp. of chili powder
- 1½ lb. of boneless pork loin chops
- 1 can (14-1/2 oz.) petite diced tomatoes, undrained
- 1 small onion, finely chopped
- 1 celery rib, chopped
- 1 small carrot, julienned
- 1 garlic clove, minced
- ½ tsp. of Louisiana-style hot sauce
- ¼ tsp. of salt
- ¾ cup of reduced-sodium chicken broth
- 1 to ½ cups of uncooked instant rice

Cooking Instructions:
1. Select the Sauté function on your Pressure Cooker and adjust for high heat, add oil.

2. Add green pepper, cook and stir for 4 to 5 minutes or until crisp-tender.

3. Remove pepper and reserve aside. Select the Cancel function to turn off Sauté function.

4. Mix cumin and chili powder, sprinkle pork chops with 2 tsp. of spice mixture.

5. Place the pork in your Pressure Cooker. In a medium bowl, mix together tomatoes, onion, celery, carrot, garlic, hot sauce, salt and remaining spice mixture.

6. Pour the mixture over pork. Secure the Lid in place and make sure vent is closed.

7. Select the Manual function, set to cook at High Pressure for about 6 minutes.

8. When the time is up, allow the cooker to release pressure naturally for about 5 minutes before doing a quick pressure release.

9. Stir in chicken broth, breaking up pork into pieces. Select the Sauté function and adjust for normal heat, bring to a boil. Add rice.

10. Cook until rice is tender, 5 minutes longer. Serve with sautéed green pepper if you desire.

11. Serve and enjoy!

Chinese-Style Ribs

Total time: 50 minutes
Preparation time: 20 min.
Cooking time: 30 minutes
Serve: 5 to 6 people

Recipe Ingredients:

- 3 lb. of boneless country-style pork ribs
- green onions, cut into 1-inch pieces
- 1 can (8 oz.) sliced water chestnuts, drained
- ¾ cup of hoisin sauce
- ½ cup of water
- 3 tbsp. of soy sauce
- 2 tbsp. of sherry or chicken stock
- 5 garlic cloves, minced
- 1 tbsp. of minced fresh gingerroot
- 1 tbsp. of light corn syrup
- 1 tbsp. of orange marmalade
- 1 tsp. of pumpkin pie spice
- ½ tsp. of crushed red pepper flakes
- 1 to 2 tbsp. of cornstarch
- 2 tbsp. of water
- Hot cooked rice, optional
- Thinly sliced / chopped green onions, optional

Cooking Instructions:

1. Place pork, green onions and water chestnuts in your Pressure Cooker.

2. In a medium bowl, Mix hoisin sauce, water, soy sauce, sherry, garlic, gingerroot, corn syrup, marmalade, pie spice and pepper flakes.

3. Pour over pork. Secure the Lid in place and make sure vent is closed. Select the Manual function, set to cook at High Pressure for about 25 minutes.

4. When the time is up, allow the cooker to release pressure naturally for about 10 minutes before doing a quick pressure release.

5. Remove pork to a serving platter; keep warm. Skim fat from cooking juices.

6. Select the Sauté function and adjust for normal heat. Bring to a boil. Mix cornstarch and water until smooth in a small bowl.

7. Gradually stir cornstarch mixture into the Pressure Cooker. Bring to a boil, cook and stir until thickened for about 2 minutes.

8. Serve ribs with sauce and, if desired, rice and additional green onions.

9. Serve and enjoy.

Thai Coconut Beef

Total time: 1 hr. 10 minutes
Preparation time: 30 min.
Cooking time: 40 minutes
Serve: 8 to 10 people

Recipe Ingredients:
- 1 boneless beef chuck roast (3 lb.), halved
- 1 tsp. of salt
- 1 tsp. of pepper
- 2 tbsp. of canola oil
- 1 large sweet red pepper, sliced
- 1 can (13.66 oz.) coconut milk
- ¾ cup of beef stock
- ½ cup of creamy peanut butter
- ¼ cup of red curry paste
- 2 tbsp. of soy sauce
- 2 tbsp. of honey
- 2 tsp. of minced fresh gingerroot
- ½ lb. of fresh sugar snap peas, trimmed
- ¼ cup of minced fresh cilantro
- Hot cooked brown or white rice

Optional toppings: thinly sliced green onions, chopped unsalted peanuts, hot sauce and lime wedges

Cooking Instructions:
1. Sprinkle beef with salt and pepper. Select the Sauté function on your Pressure Cooker and adjust for high heat.

2. Add oil; add one roast half. Brown on all sides for about 5 minutes. Remove the beef. repeat with remaining beef.

3. Return beef to your Pressure Cooker, add red pepper. Whisk coconut milk with next six ingredients in a medium bowl, pour over meat.

4. Secure the Lid in place and make sure vent is closed. Select the Manual function, set to cook at High Pressure for about 35 minutes.

5. When the time is up, do a quick pressure release. Open the Lid carefully and add sugar snap peas. Secure the Lid and make sure vent is closed.

6. Select the Manual function, set to cook at High Pressure for about 5 minutes.

7. When the time is up, allow the cooker to release pressure naturally for about 10 minutes before doing a quick pressure release.

8. Remove beef, allow beef to cool slightly. Skim fat from cooking juices. Shred beef with two forks.

9. Stir in cilantro. Serve with rice and toppings of your choice. **Freeze option:** Place cooled meat mixture in freezer containers.

10. To use, partially thaw in refrigerator overnight. Microwave, covered, on high in a microwave-safe dish until heated through, gently stirring and adding a little broth or water if necessary.

11. Serve and enjoy.

Char Siu Pork

Overall time: 1 hr. 35 minutes
Prep: 25 minutes
Cook: 1 hr. 15 minutes
Serves: 6-8 people

Recipe Ingredients:

- ½ cup of honey
- ½ cup of hoisin sauce
- ¼ cup of soy sauce
- ¼ cup of ketchup
- 4 garlic cloves, minced
- 4 tsp. of minced fresh gingerroot
- 1 tsp. of Chinese five-spice powder
- 1 boneless pork shoulder butt roast (3 to 4 lb.)
- ½ cup of chicken broth
- Fresh cilantro leaves

Cooking Instructions:

1. Combine first seven ingredients, pour into a large resealable plastic bag. Cut roast in half, add to bag and turn to coat.

2. Refrigerate overnight. Transfer the pork and marinade to your Pressure Cooker.

3. Add chicken broth. Secure the Lid in place and make sure vent is closed. Select the Manual function, set to cook at High Pressure for about 75 minutes.

4. When the time is up, allow the cooker to release pressure naturally for about 10 minutes before doing a quick pressure release.

5. Remove pork from the pot, when cool enough to handle, shred meat using two forks.

6. Skim fat from cooking juices. Return pork to your Pressure Cooker. Select the Sauté function and adjust for normal heat, heat through.

7. Top with fresh cilantro if you desire.

8. Serve immediately and enjoy!

Sicilian Meat Sauce

Total time 1 hr. 10 minutes
Preparation time: 30 min.
Cooking time: 40 minutes
Serves: 8 to 10 people

Recipe Ingredients:

- 3 tbsp. of olive oil, divided
- 2 lb. of boneless country-style pork ribs
- 1 medium onion, chopped
- 3 to 5 garlic cloves, minced
- 2 cans (28 oz. each) crushed or diced tomatoes
- 1 can (6 oz.) Italian tomato paste
- 3 bay leaves
- 2 tbsp. of chopped fresh parsley
- 2 tbsp. of chopped capers, drained
- ½ tsp. of dried basil
- ½ tsp. of dried rosemary, crushed
- ½ tsp. of dried thyme
- ½ tsp. of crushed red pepper flakes
- ½ tsp. of salt
- ½ tsp. of sugar
- 1 cup of beef broth
- ½ cup of dry red wine or additional beef broth
- Hot cooked pasta
- Grated Parmesan cheese, optional

Cooking Instructions:

1. Select the Sauté function on your Pressure Cooker and adjust for high heat, add 2 tablespoons of olive oil.

2. In batches, brown the pork on all sides and reserve aside. Add remaining oil to Pressure Cooker and Sauté onion for about 2 minutes.

3. Add in garlic and cook for 1 minute more. Add in the next 11 ingredients. Transfer the meat to Pressure Cooker.

4. Pour in broth and red wine, bring to a light boil. Secure the Lid and make sure vent is closed.

5. Select the Manual function, set to cook at High Pressure for about 35 minutes.

6. When the time is up, allow the cooker to release pressure naturally for about 10 minutes before doing a quick pressure release.

7. Discard bay leaves. Remove meat from the Pressure Cooker, pull apart, discarding bones.

8. Return meat to sauce. Serve over pasta if desire, sprinkle with Parmesan cheese.

9. Serve and enjoy.

BBQ Beef Short Ribs

Overall time: 10 minutes
Cooking time: 40 minutes
Total time: 50 minutes
Yield: 2-3 people

Recipe Ingredients:

- 8 oz. (227 g) short ribs
- Sea salt and pepper to taste
- 3 tsp. of (15 ml) olive oil, avocado oil or lard
- 1 large onion, sliced into rings
- ½ cup of (118 ml) high-quality store-bought ketchup
- ½ cup of (118 ml) crushed tomatoes
- ¼ cup of (60 ml) local honey
- Onion powder (½ tsp.)
- 1 teaspoon of (5 ml) liquid smoke
- Garlic powder (½ tsp.)
- Sea salt (½ tsp.)
- (Optional) 1 tsp. (5 ml) gluten-free Worcestershire sauce
- (Optional) Fresh thyme
- To serve: Potato Salad & Steamed Greens

Cooking Instructions:

1. Season the short ribs with sea salt and pepper. Drizzle the cooking oil into the stainless-steel bowl.

2. Switch your Instant Pot to Sauté mode, after the oil heats for about 1 minute, transfer the seasoned ribs and onions into the oil.

3. Cook the ribs on each side for about 3 minutes. In a mixing bowl combine the ketchup, tomatoes, honey, onion powder, liquid smoke, garlic powder, sea salt and Worcestershire sauce.

4. Stir thoroughly. Then pour the sauce over the ribs, secure the Lid in place and make sure the vent is sealed.

5. Select Manual button, set to cook for 28 minutes. After the 28 minutes, do a quick pressure release until the float valve drops.

6. Remove the Lid carefully and remove the ribs from the sauce. Ladle off as much of the fat as you wish to before reducing the BBQ sauce.

7. Leave a little fat. Switch your Instant Pot to Sauté mode once more and allow the sauce to simmer for about 10 minutes.

8. As it reduces, the onions and sauce could potentially stick to the bottom of the stainless-steel bowl. Shift the contents with spoon if this begins to happen.

9. Once the sauce has reached your desired texture and thickness, spoon it on top of the ribs and serve.

10. Garnish with fresh thyme if you desire.

11. Serve immediately and enjoy!

Beef Bourguignon

Preparation time: 20 minutes
Cooking time: 55 minutes
Overall time: 1 hour 15 minutes
Serves: 5-6 people

Ingredients:

- 2 medium brown onions, finely diced (or 7 to 8 small shallots, peeled and left whole)
- 4 slices of bacon or pancetta
- 1 tbsp. of olive oil
- 3 cloves of crushed or (finely diced garlic)
- 3 lbs. of (1.5 kg) good quality braising beef steak (cut into cubes)
- 1½ tsp. of sea salt
- ½ tsp. of ground black pepper
- 1 cup of stock (beef or chicken)
- 1 cup of red wine
- 1 cup of chopped tinned tomatoes
- 1 tsp. of mixed dried herbs
- 1 bay leaf
- 2 sprigs of rosemary
- (Optional) 5 oz. (150 g) button mushrooms (sliced or left whole if they are small)
- 2 large carrots (sliced)

To finish:

- 1 tbsp. of cornstarch, regular flour or tapioca flour
- 1 tbsp. of butter
- 2 tbsp. of freshly chopped parsley, to serve

Cooking Directions:

1. Peel and chop the onion and dice the bacon, Switch your Instant Pot to Sauté mode.

2. Add in olive oil, onion and bacon to the inner pot and cook for 5 minutes, stirring a few times, until golden brown.

3. Add in garlic, beef, salt, pepper, stock, red wine, tomatoes, and herbs and give everything a good stir.

4. Add mushrooms if you desire, and half of the carrots (reserve the other half for later).

5. Select Keep Warm/Cancel button to stop the Sauté function. Secure the Lid and make sure vent is closed.

6. Select Manual button, set to cook at High Pressure for 30 minutes. After the 30 minutes, allow the Pressure Cooker to release pressure naturally for 10 minutes.

7. Do a quick pressure release until the float valve drops. Add the remaining carrots. Select the Sauté function and Sauté for more 10 minutes (keep the lid off).

8. Stir a few times. This process will thicken the sauce slightly by evaporating some of the liquid.

9. Combine the cornstarch or other flour with a couple of tablespoons of water or the broth from the stew in a small mixing bowl.

10. Whisk them together and return to the broth. Stir through immediately and add the butter. Stir through to finish the dish.

11. Sprinkle with parsley when serving in bowls over your preferred side of vegetables or pasta.

12. Serve immediately and enjoy.

Chorizo Chili

Preparation time: 15 minutes
Cooking time: 20 minutes
Overall time: 35 minutes
Yield: 5-6 people
Ingredients:
- 1½ tbsp. of olive oil or coconut oil
- 1 large brown onion, roughly chopped
- 1 medium carrot or 2 small ones (peeled and diced into small cubes)
- 1 celery stick (diced into small cubes)
- 7 oz. / 200 g chorizo sausage (peeled and diced)
- 1 long red chili, finely diced
- 2.2 lb. / 1 kg ground beef (grass-fed, if possible)
- 3 cloves garlic (finely diced)
- 2 tsp. of ground cumin
- 2 tsp. of ground coriander seed
- 2 cups / about 400 g tinned chopped tomatoes
- 4 tbsp. of tomato paste
- 1 tbsp. of Tamari or soy sauce (coconut aminos for those on Whole30/paleo)
- 2 tsp. of salt
- 2 bay leaves
- 3 tbsp. of port or fortified red wine (optional but adds lots of depth)

To serve: flash pan-fried zucchini or cooked white rice, chopped avocado and cilantro.

Cooking Directions:
1. Switch your Instant Pot to Sauté mode, add in the oil, onion, carrot, celery, chorizo and chili. Cook together for 3 to 4 minutes.

2. Add in the beef, garlic, spices and stir together. Add the tinned tomatoes paste and give everything a good stir.

3. Add in the remaining ingredients and give everything a good stir. Select Keep Warm/Cancel button, to stop the Sauté function.

4. Secure the Lid in place and make sure vent is closed. Select Manual button, set to cook at High Pressure for 15 minutes.

5. After the 15 minutes, allow the Pressure Cooker to release pressure naturally for about 5 minutes before doing a quick pressure release.

6. If storing in the freezer, make sure to cool down the chili first.

7. Serve immediately and enjoy!

Picadillo

Total time: 25 minutes
Preparation time: 10 minutes
Cooking time: 15 minutes
Serves: 5 to 6 people

Recipe Ingredients:
- 1½ lbs. of 93% lean ground beef
- ½ large chopped onion
- 2 cloves garlic, minced
- 1 tomato (chopped)
- 1 tsp. of kosher salt
- ½ red bell pepper, finely chopped
- 2 tablespoons of cilantro
- 4 oz. (1/2 can) tomato sauce
- 1 tsp. ground cumin
- 1 to 2 bay leaf
- 2 tbsp. of alcaparrado (capers or green olives would work too)

Cooking Directions:
1. Switch your Instant Pot to Sauté mode, Once hot brown meat and season with salt and pepper.

2. Use a wooden spoon to break the meat up into small pieces until no longer pink. Add in onion, garlic, tomato, salt, pepper and cilantro and stir for 1 minute.

3. Add alcaparrado or olives and about 2 tablespoons of the brine, cumin, and bay leaf.

4. Add tomato sauce and 3 tbsp. of water and mix well to combine. Select Manual button, adjust time to cook at High Pressure for 15 minutes.

5. After the 15 minutes, do a quick pressure release until the float valve drops.

6. Serve immediately and enjoy.

Italian Tomato Meatballs

Preparation time: 15 minutes
Cooking time: 15 minutes
Overall time: 30 minutes
Yield: 3-4 people
Ingredients:
For the meatballs:

- 1.3 lbs. of / 600 g ground beef (beef mince)
- 1 teaspoon of onion powder
- 1 tsp. of garlic powder
- 1 tsp. of dried oregano
- 2 tsp. of ground paprika
- ½ tsp. of celery salt (optional, if not using, add ½ tsp regular salt)
- 1 tsp. of salt

For the sauce:

- 2 tbsp. of olive oil
- 1 brown onion (finely diced)
- ½ long fresh red chili, chopped (or ½ tsp red chili flakes or powder)
- 1 tsp. of salt
- 2 large garlic cloves, finely diced
- 1 can tinned diced chopped tomatoes (400 ml)

Cooking Directions:

1. Combine the ground beef with the spices and salt in a mixing bowl, mix well using clean hands.

2. Roll the mixture into small 2-inch balls and reserve aside. Switch your Instant Pot to Sauté mode.

3. Add in the olive oil, onions, chill and salt and sauté for about 5 minutes, stirring a few times.

4. Select Keep Warm/Cancel button, to stop the Sauté function. Add the meatballs and sprinkle with garlic.

5. Pour over the tinned tomatoes. Stir through and spread the meatballs evenly in the sauce. Secure the Lid and make sure vent is closed.

6. Select Manual button, adjust time to cook at High Pressure for 5 minutes. After the 5 minutes.

7. Allow the Pressure Cooker to release pressure naturally for 10 minutes before doing a quick pressure release.

8. Serve over spaghetti, rice, sliced baguettes or with a side of cauliflower rice or steamed vegetables.

9. Serve and enjoy!

Ground Beef Bulgogi

Overall time: 20 minutes
Preparation time: 10 minutes
Cooking time: 10 minutes

Ingredients:
- 2 tbsp. of oil
- 6 cloves of garlic (minced)
- 2-inch knob ginger (minced)
- 2 lbs. of ground beef
- ½ cup of coconut sugar
- ⅔ cup of coconut aminos
- 1 tsp. of crushed red pepper flakes
- 1 teaspoon of salt
- ½ tsp. of black pepper

Later:
- 6 green onions, thinly sliced
- 2 tbsp. of sesame oil
- 2 tsp. of sesame seeds

Cooking Directions:
1. In your Instant Pot, add the oil, garlic and ginger. Switch your Instant Pot to Sauté mode. Sauté for 2 to 3 minutes.

2. Add the ground beef to the pot and cook until mostly brown. Add the remaining of the ingredients to the pot and mix well together.

3. Secure the Lid in place and make sure vent is closed. Select Manual button, adjust time to cook at High Pressure for 10 minutes.

4. After the 10 minutes, do a quick pressure release until the float valve drops. If the meat released a lot of liquid.

5. Select the sauté button to boil off any extra liquid. Stir the green onions, sesame oil and sesame seeds into the pot.

6. Serve immediately and enjoy!

Kalua Pork

Preparation time: 6 minutes
Cooking time: 1 hour 14 minutes
Overall time: 1 hour 20 minutes
Serves: 4-5 people

Ingredients:
- 4 lbs. of (1614g) pork shoulder (pork butt meat), cut into 2 to 2¼ inches cubes
- 1 cup of (250ml) cold water
- 1 tbsp. of (17g) coarse alaea red Hawaiian sea salt
- 1 tbsp. of (15ml) liquid smoke
- 2 pieces (90g) 12x20 inches banana leaves

Cooking Instructions:
1. Cut the pork into 2 to 2¼ inches cubes and place them in a mixing bowl.

2. Add 1 tablespoon of (17g) coarse alaea Hawaiian sea salt & 1 tablespoon (15ml) liquid smoke.

3. Mix very well, marinate for 30 minutes. Pour in 1 cup of (250ml) cold water in your Instant Pot.

4. Layer a banana leaf at the bottom, then add in cubed pork. Try fitting the pork in a singer layer so they are partially submerged in the water.

5. Then, layer another banana leaf on top of the pork. Select Manual button, adjust time to cook at High Pressure for 45 minutes.

6. After the 45 minutes, allow the Pressure Cooker to release pressure naturally for 15 minutes.

7. Discard the top banana leaf and check if the pork is tenderized. If the pork is still tough, pressure cook for another 10 minutes more.

8. Use two forks to shred Kalua pork. Taste and season with more alaea Hawaiian sea salt if needed.

9. Serve immediately and enjoy!

Boneless Pork Chops

Preparation time: 10 minutes
Cooking time: 7 minutes
Overall time: 17 minutes
Serves: 2-3 people

Ingredients:

- 2 pork chops, (boneless 1" thick)
- 2 tablespoons of brown sugar
- 1 tsp. of salt
- 1 tsp. of black pepper
- 1 tsp. of paprika
- ½ tsp. of onion powder
- 1 tbsp. of butter
- 1 cup of chicken broth
- ½ tbsp. of Worcestershire sauce
- 1 tsp. of liquid smoke

Cooking Directions:

1. Mix spices and brown sugar, rub into both sides of pork chops. Switch your Instant Pot to Sauté mode and adjust for high heat. Add 1 tbsp. of butter.

2. Once hot, add pork chops and brown on both sides for 1 to 2 minutes each. Remove pork chops and reserve aside.

3. Select Warm/Cancel button, to stop the Sauté function. Add 1 cup of chicken broth.

4. Use a wooden spoon to deglaze the bits off the bottom of the pot. Add Worcestershire sauce and liquid smoke.

5. Add pork chops directly to the pot in the liquid. Secure the Lid in place and make sure vent is sealed.

6. Select Manual button, adjust time set to cook for about 7 minutes. After the 7 minutes.

7. Allow the Pressure Cooker to release pressure naturally for 12 minutes before doing a quick pressure release. Remove the Lid and pork chops.

8. Let pork chops rest for about 5 minutes before serving.

9. Serve immediately and enjoy!

Pork Chops with Bacon Apple Glaze

Preparation time: 10 minutes
Cooking time: 20 minutes
Overall time: 30 minutes
Serves: 6 pork chops

Ingredients:

- 3 slices thick cut bacon diced
- Onion diced (½)
- 1 tsp. of minced garlic
- ¼ tsp. of dried thyme
- Dried parsley (½ tsp.)
- ½ teaspoon of salt
- Pinch of black pepper
- 2 tbsp. of canola oil
- Salt and pepper
- 6 boneless thick cut pork chops
- 1 cup unsweetened apple juice
- 1 tbsp. of corn starch
- 1 tbsp. of water

Cooking Instructions:

1. Switch your Instant Pot to Sauté mode and wait until it reads Hot.

2. Add the bacon and onion and cook, stirring often, until bacon is crispy and onion has softened and browned.

3. Then add in the garlic, thyme, parsley, salt and pepper. Stir together and remove from the pot with a slotted spoon, leaving the bacon grease behind.

4. Drizzle oil over both sides of the pork chops. Season the pork chops with salt and pepper.

5. Sear on both sides in a single layer, in the Instant Pot, until browned and they move easily.

6. (If they feel stuck, they are probably not quite done). You may have to sear the chops in two sets.

7. Turn the Instant Pot off. Add the apple juice to the hot pan, and use a wooden spoon to deglaze the bottom of the pan.

8. Secure the Lid and make sure vent is closed. Select Manual button, adjust time to cook at High pressure for 8 minutes.

9. After the 8 minutes, allow the Pressure Cooker to release pressure naturally for about 10 minutes before doing a quick pressure release.

10. Remove the Lid carefully. Remove the pork chops to a plate and cover to keep warm.

11. Switch your Instant Pot to Sauté mode. Combine cornstarch and water and add the juices in pot, along with the bacon and onion, cooking and stirring to thicken.

12. Serve over pork chops and enjoy!

CHAPTER 5: PASTA & SIDE DISHES

Not-Fried Pinto Beans

Overall time: 1 hour
Preparation time: 5 minutes
Cooking time: 55 minutes
Ingredients:
- 1 cup of dried pinto beans (soaked for 8 hours and drained)
- Water (3 cups)
- ½ yellow onion, chopped
- 2 cloves garlic, minced
- 1 teaspoon of ground cumin
- 1 tsp. of chili powder
- ¼ tsp. of freshly ground black pepper
- (Optional) pinch of cayenne pepper
- ½ to ¾ tsp. of fine sea salt

Optional garnish: Chopped fresh cilantro, Lime wedges, diced tomato, sliced jalapeño, diced avocado

Cooking Directions:
1. In your Instant Pot, combine the drained beans, water, onion, and garlic. Stir together.

2. Make sure the beans are submerged. Secure the Lid in place and make sure vent is closed.

3. Select Manual button, adjust time to cook at High Pressure for 20 minutes. After the 20 minutes.

4. Allow the Pressure Cooker to release pressure naturally for 10 minutes before doing a quick pressure release.

5. Remove the Lid carefully and drain the beans, reserving the liquid. Return the cooked beans to the Instant Pot.

6. Stir in ½ cup of the reserved cooking liquid, along with the cumin, chili powder, black pepper, cayenne, and ½ tsp. of salt.

7. Use a potato masher to mash the cooked beans until smooth, leaving some texture if you desire.

8. Taste and season with salt if necessary. Serve warm with a garnish of cilantro and a squeeze of lime juice.

9. Store leftover beans in an airtight container in the fridge for 1 week.

10. Serve and enjoy!

Rigatoni with Sausage & Peas

Preparation time: 10 minutes

Cooking time: 15 minutes

Overall time: 30 min.

Serves: 5-6 people

Recipe Ingredients:

- 1 lb. of Johnsonville ground mild Italian sausage
- 4 garlic cloves, minced
- ¼ cup of tomato paste
- 12 oz. uncooked rigatoni or large tube pasta
- 1-1/2 cups of frozen peas
- 1 can (28 oz.) crushed tomatoes
- ½ tsp. of dried basil
- ¼ to ½ tsp. of crushed red pepper flakes
- 4 cups of water
- ½ cup of heavy whipping cream
- ½ cup of crumbled goat or feta cheese
- Thinly sliced fresh basil, (optional)

Cooking Instructions

1. Switch your Instant Pot to Sauté mode and adjust for high heat.

2. Cook and crumble sausage until no longer pink for about 4 to 6 minutes. Add in garlic and cook for 1 minute longer.

3. Add tomato paste, cook and stir until meat is coated for 1 to 2 minutes. Stir in the next five ingredients.

4. Pour in water and secure the Lid, make sure vent is closed. Select Manual button, adjust time to cook at Low Pressure for 6 minutes.

5. After 6 minutes, do a quick pressure release and stir in cream, heat through.

6. Top with cheese and, if desired, fresh basil.

7. Serve and enjoy!

Buffalo Shrimp Mac & Cheese

Overall time: 25 minutes
Preparation time: 15 minutes
Cooking time: 10 minutes
Serves: 5-6 people

Recipe Ingredients:

- 2 cups 2% milk
- 1 cup half-and-half cream
- 1 tbsp. of unsalted butter
- 1 tsp. of ground mustard
- ½ tsp. of onion powder
- ¼ tsp. of white pepper
- ¼ tsp. of ground nutmeg
- 1-1/2 cups of uncooked elbow macaroni
- 2 cups of shredded cheddar cheese
- 1 cup of shredded Gouda or Swiss cheese
- ¾ lb. of frozen cooked salad shrimp, thawed
- 1 cup of crumbled blue cheese
- 2 tbsp. of Louisiana-style hot sauce
- 2 tbsp. of minced fresh chives
- 2 tbsp. of minced fresh parsley
- Additional Louisiana-style hot sauce, optional

Cooking Instructions:

1. In your Pressure Cooker, combine the first seven ingredients, stir in macaroni.

2. Secure the Lid in place and make sure vent is closed. Select Manual button, adjust time to cook at High Pressure for 3 minutes.

3. When the time is up, allow the cooker to release pressure naturally for about 4 minutes before doing a quick pressure release.

4. Select the Sauté function and adjust for normal heat. Stir in shredded cheeses, shrimp, blue cheese and hot sauce.

5. Cook until heated through, for 5 to 6 minutes. Just before serving.

6. Stir in chives, parsley and additional hot sauce if you desire.

7. Serve and enjoy.

Mac and Cheese

Preparation time: 10 minutes
Cooking time: 40 minutes
Total time: 50 minutes
Serves: 4 to 5 people

Recipe Ingredients:

- 16 oz. (454 g) of elbow macaroni
- 4 cups (1 L) of cold running water
- 4 tbsp. (60 g) unsalted butter
- 14 oz. (397 g) sharp cheddar, freshly grated
- 6 oz. (170 g) mild cheddar or American cheese, freshly grated
- Kosher salt and ground black pepper

Wet Ingredients:

- 2 large eggs, beaten
- 12 oz. (355 ml) can evaporated milk
- 1 tsp. (5 ml) of Sriracha sauce or Frank's hot sauce
- 1 tsp. (2 g) of ground mustard
- Bacon Bits & Scallion
- 4 to 8 strips bacon
- 2 stalks scallion, finely chopped
- Buttery Crispy Breadcrumbs
- ½ cup (31 g) panko breadcrumbs
- 1 tbsp. (15 ml) olive oil
- 1 tbsp. (15 g) unsalted butter
- Kosher salt to taste

Cooking Instructions:

1. Place bacon on a baking sheet lined with parchment paper. Then place it on the middle rack of a preheated 400°F oven.

2. Bake bacon until crispy and golden brown for about 18 to 20 minutes. Place them on a paper towel to absorb the excess fat. Cut into bacon bits.

3. Add in 16 oz. (454 g) of elbow macaroni, 4 cups (1 L) of water, and a pinch of kosher salt into the Pressure Cooker.

4. Secure the Lid and make sure vent is closed. Select the Manual function, set to cook at High Pressure for about 4 minutes.

5. When the time is up, do a quick pressure release. There is a slight chance that a tiny amount of foam will come out with the steam. Have a towel handy just in case.

6. Remove the Lid carefully. While the macaroni is pressure cooking, heat a skillet over medium heat.

7. Add 1 tbsp. (15 g) of unsalted butter, 1 tbsp. (15 ml) of olive oil, and ½ cup (31 g) of panko breadcrumbs to the skillet.

8. Toast the breadcrumbs until golden brown. Taste and add kosher salt for seasoning if necessary.

9. In a medium mixing bowl, beat 2 large eggs and mix in 1 teaspoon (2 g) of ground mustard, 1 teaspoon (5 ml) of Sriracha, and 12 oz. (355 ml) of evaporated milk. Mix well.

10. Select the Keep Warm function, give it a quick stir and see if there is excessive liquid in the pot. Drain if necessary.

11. Place 4 tbsp. (60 g) of unsalted butter into the pressure-cooked macaroni. Mix well with a silicone spatula and let the butter melt.

12. Pour in the wet ingredients and mix well. Add the grated cheese ⅓ portion at a time and stir continuously until the cheese fully melt.

13. If the mac and cheese is too runny, use Sauté Less function - Click cancel, Sauté and Adjust button twice) to reduce it down.

14. Taste and season with kosher salt and ground black pepper if necessary. You will probably need quite a few pinches of kosher salt to brighten the dish.

15. Generously sprinkle crispy breadcrumb, bacon bits, then scallion over a bowl of macaroni & cheese.

16. Serve immediately and enjoy!

Brown Sugar Baked Beans

Overall time: 35 minutes
Preparation time:10 minutes
Cooking time:25 minutes

Ingredients:

- 1 yellow onion, finely diced
- oz. can kidney beans, rinsed and drained (1¾ cups)
- ounce can pinto beans, rinsed and drained (1¾ cups)
- oz. can northern beans, rinsed and drained (1¾ cups)
- ½ cup of ketchup
- Water (¾ cup)
- 1/3 cup of dark brown sugar, unpacked
- 1 tbsp. of yellow mustard
- 1 tsp. of chili powder

Cooking Directions:

1. Add the ingredients to the Instant Pot and stir together.

2. Secure the Lid in place and select Manual button, adjust time to cook at High pressure 8 minutes.

3. After the 8 minutes, allow the Pressure Cooker to release pressure naturally for about 10 to 15 minutes before doing a quick pressure release.

4. Stir before serving. Serve immediately and enjoy!

Pizza Pasta

Preparation time: 10 minutes
Cooking time: 10 minutes
Overall time: 30 minutes
Serves: 5-6 people

Ingredients:
- Butter (2 tbsp.)
- 1 yellow onion diced
- 1 lb. of ground beef
- Minced garlic (1 tbsp.)
- Tomato paste (1 tbsp.)
- ½ tsp. of red pepper flakes
- ½ tsp. of salt
- ½ tsp. of ground black pepper
- 1 cup of tomato sauce or pizza sauce
- 5 oz. pepperoni slices
- 2 ½ cups of beef broth
- 8 oz. cellentani pasta
- 2 cups of Four Cheeses mix

Garnish: Parsley

Cooking Directions:
1. Switch your Instant Pot to Sauté mode, once Hot, melt the butter. Add the diced onion and cook for 1 to 2 minutes, stirring occasionally.

2. Add the ground beef, to get a nice sear on it. Break it up using a wooden spoon as it cooks.

3. When the ground beef is done cooked, with minimal red spots. Now add minced garlic, tomato paste, red pepper flakes, salt and pepper, stir and cook for 1 to 2 minutes.

4. Add in the tomato sauce and pepperoni. Stir together to combine. Add the beef broth and deglaze the bottom of the pot using a wooden spoon.

5. Add pasta and stir to combine. Secure the Lid in place and make sure vent is closed.

6. Select Manual button, adjust time to cook at High Pressure for 5 minutes. After the 5 minutes.

7. Do a quick pressure release until the float valve drops. Remove the Lid carefully and stir the pasta.

8. Top with the cheese, place the Lid back on but don't seal. Let it sit for 1 or 2 minutes for the cheese to start melting.
9. Then stir to combine. Serve topped with chopped parsley.

10. Serve immediately and enjoy!

Cheesesteak Pasta

Preparation time: 10 minutes
Cooking time: 5 minutes
Overall time: 15 minutes

Ingredients:

- 1 lb. of ground beef
- Butter (2 tbsp.)
- 1 yellow onion diced
- 1 tbsp. of minced garlic
- 1 green bell pepper diced
- 8 oz. baby Bella mushrooms minced
- Ketchup (2 tbsp.)
- Worcestershire sauce (1 tbsp.)
- ½ tsp. of Kosher salt
- ½ tsp. of fresh ground black pepper
- 2½ cups of beef broth
- 8 oz. shell pasta I used large shells
- 2 cups shredded cheese provolone, Swiss or mozzarella cheese

Cooking Directions:

1. Switch your Instant Pot to Sauté mode, once it is Hot melt the butter.

2. Add the ground beef, allow it to cook without moving for 1 minutes, to get a nice sear on it. After that.

3. Break it up using a wooden spoon as it cooks. Once the ground beef has browned, add in salt, pepper and Worcestershire sauce.

4. Stir together and add in onion, garlic, green pepper and mushrooms. Stir and cook for another 1 to 2 minutes.

5. Add the ketchup and beef broth. Give everything a good stir to combine. Scrape the bottom of the pot with a wooden spoon to remove bits. To avoid burning.

6. Then add in pasta and stir to combine. Secure the Lid and make sure vent is closed.

7. Select Manual button, adjust time to cook at High Pressure for 5 minutes. After the 5 minutes.

8. Do a quick pressure release until the float valve drops. Remove the Lid carefully and stir.

9. Turn off the Instant Pot. Top with cheese, place the lid back on but don't seal.

10. Allow it to sit for 1 or 2 minutes for cheese to melt. Stir to combine.

11. Serve and enjoy!

Taco Pasta

Preparation time: 10 minutes
Cooking time: 10 minutes
Overall time: 30 minutes
Serves: 5-6 people

Ingredients:
- Canola oil (2 tbsp.)
- 1 lb. of ground beef
- 1 yellow onion, diced
- Minced garlic (1 tbsp.)
- 1 tbsp. of Worcestershire sauce
- 1 to 2 tbsp. of Taco seasoning depends how you like it
- 1 tsp. of red pepper flakes
- 1 cup of chunky salsa medium spice
- 2 cups of beef broth
- 8 oz. shell pasta (we used medium shells)
- 2 cups of shredded cheddar cheese or Mexican blend cheese

Cooking Directions:
1. Switch the Instant Pot to Sauté mode, once it is Hot, add the oil and wait for it to start simmering.

2. Add the ground beef, allow it to cook without moving for 1 minute, to get a nice sear on it.

3. Break it up using a wooden spoon as it cooks. when the ground beef has browned.

4. Add in the chopped onion and minced garlic, stir and cook for 1 to 2 minutes. Add Worcestershire sauce, taco seasoning and red pepper flakes.

5. Stir and cook for another 1 to 2 minutes. Add the salsa and stir, add beef broth and stir to combine.

6. Deglaze the bottom of your pot using a wooden spoon, to make sure bits are not stuck to it.

7. Add pasta and stir to combine. Secure the Lid in place and make sure vent is sealed.

8. Select Manual button, adjust time to cook at High Pressure for 5 minutes. After the 5 minutes.

9. Do a quick pressure release until the float valve drops. Remove the Lid carefully and stir.

10. Turn off the Instant Pot and top with shredded cheese. Place the Lid back on, but don't seal.

11. Allow it to sit for 1 or 2 minutes to melt. Stir together to combine. Serve with sour cream, fresh salsa, jalapeños, avocado and fresh cilantro if you like.

12. Serve immediately and enjoy!

Chicken Pot Pie Pasta

Preparation time: 10 minutes
Cooking time: 10 minutes
Overall time: 30 minutes
Serves: 3-4 people

Ingredients:

- 3 tbsp. of canola oil or olive oil
- 1 lb. of chicken breast meat or boneless chicken thighs (cut into 1 to 2-inch cubes)
- 1 small onion, diced
- Minced garlic (1 tbsp.)
- (Optional) ½ tsp. of salt
- ¼ tsp. of ground black pepper optional
- ¼ tsp. of red pepper flakes
- 1 ½ cups of chicken broth low sodium
- 3 cups of wide egg noodles uncooked
- ½ cup of water
- 1 cup of sour cream
- 10 oz. mixed veggies, frozen (we used a mix of beans, peas, carrots and corn)

Cornstarch Slurry:

- ¼ cup of corn-starch
- ¼ cup of water

Cooking Directions:

1. Switch the Sauté button, once the Instant Pot is Hot, add the oil.

2. Add the diced onion and minced garlic and cook for 1 to 2 minutes, stirring occasionally.

3. Add the cubes chicken and cook until no longer pink, stir occasionally for about 3 minutes.

4. Add salt, pepper and red pepper flakes. Stir together to combine. Then add the chicken broth.

5. Add uncooked pasta to the pot and gently push it using a wooden spoon so its evenly distributed and submerged in the liquid.

6. Add ½ cup of water over pasta. Secure the Lid in place and make sure vent is closed.

7. Select Manual button, adjust time to cook at High Pressure for 4 minutes. After the 4 minutes.

8. Allow the Pressure Cooker to release pressure naturally for 4 minutes before doing a quick pressure release.

9. Carefully remove Lid and stir. Switch your Instant Pot to Sauté mode, add the frozen veggies and sour cream.

10. Stir together to combine and cook for 2 minutes. In a small mixing bowl, mix cornstarch and water until fully combined. Add to the pot.

11. Gently stir to combine and cook for about 1 to 2 minutes, until it thickens. Turn off the Instant Pot.

12. Serve topped with chopped parsley if you like.

13. Serve immediately and enjoy!

Creamy Mac and Cheese

Preparation time: 5 minutes
Cooking time: 5 minutes
Overall time: 10 minutes
Serves: 5-6 people

Ingredients:

Cook the Pasta:
- 1 lb. of elbow macaroni dry
- 4 tbsp. of butter unsalted
- 4 ½ cups of water
- Dry mustard (1 tsp.)
- Thyme (½ tsp.)
- ¼ tsp. of ground black pepper
- ¼ tsp. of kosher salt
- ½ tsp. of garlic powder
- (Optional) ¼ tsp. of red pepper flakes

Cheese:
- 4 oz. cream cheese softened and cubed
- 1 cup of milk warm
- ½ cup of heavy whipping cream warm
- 2 to 3 cups of cheddar cheese shredded
- 1 cup of parmesan shredded

Garnish:
- (Optionalo 10 slices thick cut cooked bacon

Cooking Directions:
1. Add all the ingredients from the "Cook the Pasta" list to the pot and stir together to combine.

2. Secure the Lid in place and make sure vent is closed. Select Manual button, adjust time to cook at High Pressure for 5 minutes.

3. After the 5 minutes, do a quick pressure release until the float valve drops. Remove the Lid carefully and stir together.

4. Switch your Instant Pot to Warm mode, add the cream cheese, warm milk, warm cream, 2 cups of cheddar cheese and parmesan cheese until fully melted.

5. Stir in the remaining 1 cup of shredded cheddar cheese if you desire. If the sauce is too thick you can stir in more warm milk.

6. Turn off Instant Pot. Top Mac and cheese with cooked bacon before serving if you desire. Serve immediately and enjoy!

Cauliflower Tikka Masala

Serves: 3-4 people
Recipe Ingredients:
- 1 tbsp. of vegan butter (or oil)
- 1 medium onion, diced
- 3 cloves of garlic (minced)
- 1 tbsp. of freshly grated ginger
- 2 tsp. of dried fenugreek leaves
- 2 tsp. of garam masala
- 1 tsp. of turmeric
- Ground chili (½ tsp.)
- ¼ tsp. of ground cumin
- Salt (½ tsp.)
- 1 28-oz. can crushed tomatoes
- 1 tbsp. maple syrup
- 1 cauliflower head, cut into florets
- ½ cup of non-dairy yogurt (or cashew cream)

Optional toppings: fresh parsley, roasted cashews

Cooking Directions:
1. Select the Sauté button and wait for 7 minutes, add in the oil. Once Hot, add the onion, garlic, and ginger.

2. Cook for 3 to 4 minutes, add the dried fenugreek leaves, garam masala, turmeric, chili, cumin, and salt.

3. Continue to cook for another 2 minutes, stirring regularly to make sure it doesn't burn.

4. Add the crushed tomatoes, maple syrup, and cauliflower florets. Secure the lid in place and make sure vent is closed.

5. Select Manual button, adjust time to cook for 2 minutes. After the 2 minutes.

6. Allow the cooker to release pressure naturally for 1 minute before doing a quick pressure release.

7. Stir in the non-dairy yogurt and stir to combine. Serve hot with rice, naan, or tofu.

8. Top with fresh parsley and roasted cashews.

9. Serve immediately enjoy!

Tomato White Beans

Preparation time: 10 minutes
Cooking time: 40 minutes
Overall time: 50 minutes
Serves: 6-7 people

Ingredients:
- 4 slices bacon (chopped)
- 1 medium yellow onion (chopped)
- 2 cloves garlic, minced
- 1 bay leaf
- ½ tsp. of kosher salt
- 2 ¼ cups of dry cannellini beans
- 28 oz. RedPack whole peeled plum tomatoes
- 6 oz. RedPack tomato paste
- 2 cups of chicken broth
- crumbled feta, fresh oregano for garnish

Cooking Instructions:
1. Press the Sauté button, allow it to heat up, once hot, add the bacon and cook until fat is rendered and bacon starts to brown.

2. Add in the onions and garlic and continue cooking until softened. Select the Cancel button, to stop the Sauté.

3. Add the bay leaf, salt, beans, tomatoes, tomato paste and chicken broth. Give everything a good stir to combine.

4. Secure the Lid in place and make sure vent is closed. Select Manual function, set to cook for about 40 minutes. When the time is up, allow the cooker to release pressure naturally for few minutes.

5. Remove the Lid carefully, stir the mixture to break down the tomatoes. Taste and season with salt and pepper if necessary.

6. Serve beans over toasted bread and top with crumbled feta and fresh oregano.

7. Serve immediately and enjoy!

Garlic Herb Mashed Potatoes

Preparation time: 12 minutes
Cooking time: 8 minutes
Overall time: 20 minutes

Ingredients:

- 2 ¼ lbs. of russet potatoes
- 3 cups of water
- 1 ½ tsp. of salt (plus more to taste)
- 6 whole cloves garlic, peeled
- 1 sprig fresh rosemary + a small bunch of thyme sprigs
- ¼ cup of butter, melted
- ¼ cup of sour cream
- 4 oz. cream cheese

For topping: chopped chives or parsley,

Cooking Directions:

1. Peel the potatoes and chop them into 4 to 6 pieces. If each of your potatoes weighs a pound, chop them into 8 pieces.

2. Add in the potatoes, water, salt, garlic, rosemary, and thyme into your Instant Pot.

3. Secure the Lid in place and make sure the vent is closed. Select Manual button, adjust time to cook at High Pressure for about 8 minutes.

4. After 8 minutes, do a quick pressure release until the float valve drops. drain the potatoes, and discard the herb sprigs. You can keep the garlic or toss it out.

5. Use a potato masher to break down the potatoes. Use a rubber spatula, mix in the melted butter, sour cream, and cream cheese.

6. Taste and adjust salt to preference. Plate and serve with chopped chives on top.

7. Serve immediately and enjoy!

Hummus (No Soak)

Preparation time: 25 minutes
Cooking time: 35 minutes
Overall time: 1 hour
Serves: 10-11 people

Ingredients:

Beans:

- 1 lb. of dried garbanzo beans, rinsed
- 12 cups of filtered water

Hummus:

- 3 cups cooked garbanzo beans, still warm
- ½ cup warm bean cooking liquid
- ¼ cup of tahini
- 2 medium cloves garlic
- 1 large lemon juiced
- 1 tsp. of kosher salt
- ½ teaspoon of ground cumin
- ¼ tsp. of smoked paprika
- ¼ cup extra virgin olive oil highest quality

Cooking Directions:

To Cook the Beans:

1. First rinse garbanzo beans and discard any stones. Place in Instant Pot, insert along with 12 cups of filtered water.

2. Secure the Lid in place and make sure vent is closed. Select Manual button, adjust time to cook for 35 minutes.

3. After 35 minutes, allow the Pressure Cooker to release pressure naturally for 15 minutes before doing a quick pressure release.

4. Carefully drain the beans, making sure to reserve the liquid.

Hummus:

1. Transfer 3 cups of warm drained, cooked garbanzo beans to the bowl of food processor fitted with the chopping blade.

2. Add in all other ingredients in your Instant Pot (Except olive oil). process until smooth and slowly add the olive in through the tube, 1 T at a time.

3. Hummus should be smooth, creamy and taste almost whipped.

4. Serve topped with Za'atar, smoked paprika and a splash of olive oil.

5. Serve immediately and enjoy.

Risotto with Peas and Artichokes

Overall time: 35 minutes
Preparation time: 10 minutes
Cooking time: 25 minutes
Serves: 3-4 people

Ingredients:

- 2 tbsp. of extra virgin olive oil
- 1 small yellow onion (peeled and diced)
- 3 cloves garlic, minced
- 1½ cups of arborio, carnaroli, or vialone rice
- 4 cups of vegetable stock
- 1 ½ cups of frozen peas, thawed
- 1 (12 oz.) jar artichoke hearts, drained
- salt, to taste
- freshly ground black pepper, to taste
- (Optional) ¼ cup of nutritional yeast or a pinch of truffle salt
- (Optional) fresh Italian parsley or basil, for garnish

Cooking Instructions:

1. Press the Sauté button and heat up the olive oil. Add the onion and Sauté until tender and golden brown, for 4 to 5 minutes.

2. Add the garlic and Sauté another minute longer. Add the rice and stir to toast for about 1 minute.

3. Add the vegetable stock. Secure the Lid in place and make sure vent is closed.

4. Select Manual button, adjust time to cook for 5 minutes. After 5 minutes, do a quick pressure release until the float valve drops.

5. Remove the Lid and stir the risotto. Add more broth if needed to loosen it up. Stir in the peas and artichokes.

6. Taste and season with salt and pepper if necessary. Secure the Lid in place and wait for a few minutes to heat up the peas and artichokes.

7. Stir again and season to taste with salt and pepper, and nutritional yeast, if using.

8. Serve immediately and enjoy!

CHAPTER 6: APPETIZERS

Cheddar Bacon Ale Dip

Overall time: 25 minutes
Preparation: 15 minutes.
Cooking: 10 minutes.
Makes: 4½ cups

Ingredients:

- 18 oz. cream cheese, softened
- ¼ cup of sour cream
- 1½ tbsp. of Dijon mustard
- 1 tsp. of garlic powder
- 1 cup of beer or non-alcoholic beer
- 1 lb. of bacon strips (cooked and crumbled)
- 2 cups of shredded cheddar cheese
- ¼ cup of heavy whipping cream
- 1 green onion, thinly sliced
- Soft pretzel bites

Cooking Directions:

1. In your pressure cooker, combine cream cheese, sour cream, mustard and garlic powder until smooth.

2. Stir in beer. Add bacon, reserving 2 tbsp. Secure the Lid in place and make sure vent is closed.

3. Select Manual button, set to cook at High Pressure for 5 minutes. After the 5 minutes.

4. Do a quick pressure release until the float valve drops. Select the Sauté function, adjust for normal heat.

5. Stir in cheese and heavy cream. Cook and stir until mixture has thickened for about 3 to 4 minutes.

6. Transfer to serving dish. Sprinkle with onion and reserved bacon.

7. Serve with pretzel bun bites and enjoy!

Beer-Braised Pulled Ham

Overall time: 35 minutes
Preparation time: 10 minutes.
Cooking time: 25 minutes
Makes: 16 servings

Ingredients:

- 2 bottles of (12 oz. each) beer or nonalcoholic beer
- ¾ cup of German or Dijon mustard, divided
- ½ tsp. of coarsely ground pepper
- 1 fully cooked bone-in ham (4 lbs.)
- 4 fresh rosemary sprigs
- 16 pretzel hamburger buns, split
- (Optional) Dill pickle slices

Cooking Directions:

1. In your pressure cooker, whisk together beer, ½ cup of mustard and pepper. Add ham and rosemary.

2. Secure the Lid in place and make sure vent is sealed. Select Manual button, adjust time to cook at High Pressure for 20 minutes.

3. After the 20 minutes, allow the Pressure Cooker to release pressure naturally for 10 minutes.

4. Do a quick pressure release until float valve drops. Remove ham from pot, cool slightly.

5. Discard rosemary sprigs. Skim fat from liquid remaining in pressure cooker. Switch your Instant Pot to Sauté mode. set to cook at High Pressure for 5 minutes.

6. When ham is cool enough to handle, use two forks to shred the meat. Discard bone. Return ham to pressure cooker; heat through.

7. To serve, place shredded ham on pretzel bun bottoms with remaining mustard and, if desired, dill pickle slices. Replace tops.

8. Serve immediately and enjoy!

Buffalo Ranch Chicken Dip

Preparation time: 5 minutes
Cooking time: 15 minutes
Overall time: 20 minutes
Serves: 5-6 people

Recipe Ingredients:

- 1 lb. of chicken breast
- 1 packet ranch dip
- 1 cup of Hot Sauce
- 1 stick butter
- 16 oz. cheddar cheese
- 8 oz. cream cheese

Cooking Directions:

1. Place chicken, cream cheese, butter, hot sauce, and a packet of Ranch dip in the Instant Pot.

2. Select Manual button, adjust time to cook at High Pressure for 15 minutes. After the 15 minutes.

3. Do a quick pressure release until float valve drops. Shred chicken with fork.

4. Stir in cheddar cheese. Serve with chips and enjoy!

Prosciutto-wrapped Asparagus Canes

Preparation time: 5 minutes
Cooking time: 7 minutes
Overall time: 12 minutes

Ingredients:
- 1lb (500g) thick Asparagus
- 8oz (225g) thinly sliced Prosciutto

Cooking Directions.
1. Add 1 to 2 cups of water to your Instant Pot and set aside.

2. Wrap the asparagus spears in prosciutto. Lay any extra un-wrapped spears in a single layer along the bottom of the steamer basket.

3. Lay the prosciutto-wrapped asparagus on top in a single layer, too. Place the basket inside the pressure cooker.

4. Secure the Lid in place and make sure vent is closed. Turn the heat up high and when the pan reaches pressure, lower the heat and count 2 to 3 minutes cooking time at High Pressure.

5. When time is up, do a quick pressure release until the float valve drops. Remove the steamer basket immediately.

6. Place the asparagus on a serving platter so they are no longer cooked by residual heat from the pressure cooker.

7. Serve immediately and enjoy!

Cocktail Meatballs

Preparation time: 5 minutes
Cooking time: 5 minutes
Overall time: 10 minutes
Serves 16 servings

Ingredients:

- 2 lb. of meatballs pre-cooked frozen
- Brown sugar (¼ cup)
- Honey (¼ cup)
- ½ cup of ketchup
- 2 tbsp. of soy sauce
- 1 tablespoon of garlic minced
- ¼ cup of green onions sliced thin for garnish

Cooking Directions:

1. Combine brown sugar, honey, ketchup, soy sauce, and garlic in your pressure cooker.

2. Press the Sauté button and stir to combine. Once the mixture comes to a boil, add the frozen fully cooked meatballs.

3. Secure the Lid in place and make sure vent is sealed. Select Manual button, adjust time to cook at High Pressure for 5 minutes.

4. After the 5 minutes, allow the pressure cooker to release pressure naturally.

5. Serve immediately and enjoy!

Pizza Pull Apart Bread

Ingredients:
- 2 cans pizza dough
- 1/3 cup of olive oil
- 2 cups of mozzarella cheese
- 2 tbsp. of fresh parsley (chopped)
- 4 cloves garlic minced
- 1 pack mini pepperonis
- pizza sauce for dipping

Cooking Directions:
1. Cut pizza dough into 1-inch strips, then about 1 to 2-inch sections. (We used a pizza cutter)

2. In a medium mixing bowl, Combine the ingredients. Use your hands to toss all ingredients.

3. Place into springform pan. Add 1 cup of water to the bottom of your Instant Pot. Drop your pan in.

4. Select Manual button, adjust time to cook at High Pressure for 10 minutes.

5. After the 10 minutes, do a quick pressure release until the float valve drops.

6. Serve immediately and enjoy!

Pizza Pull Apart Bread

Bacon Cheeseburger Dip

Ingredients:
- ½ lb. of lean ground beef
- 4 to 5 slices of bacon (cut into bite sized pieces)
- 10 oz. can diced tomatoes with green chile peppers
- 8 oz. cream cheese (cut into cubes)
- 8 oz. shredded Cheddar-Monterey Jack cheese
- 4 tbsp. of water

Cooking Directions:
1. Press the Sauté button and wait until it displays Hot.

2. Add bacon pieces and cook until browned. Scoop out and place on plate lined with paper towel.

3. Throw in ground beef and cook until no longer pink. Turn off pot and drain off excess grease.

4. Add bacon, water, diced tomatoes, and cream cheese back into the pot. (Do Not Stir).

5. Secure the Lid in place and ensure that the steam valve is on sealing position.

6. Select Manual button, adjust time to cook at High Pressure for 4 minutes. After the 4 minutes.

7. Do a quick pressure release until the float valve drops. Remove the Lid carefully and stir in cheese.

8. Keep stirring until everything is well combined. Place in bowl and serve with tortilla chips.

9. Serve immediately and enjoy!

Salsa Recipe

Preparation time: 12 minutes
Cooking time: 30 minutes
Overall time: 42 minutes

Ingredients:

- 12 cups of diced, peeled & seeded fresh tomatoes
- 2 Medium green peppers (chopped and diced)
- 3 large yellow onions (chopped and diced)
- 1 cup of seeded & chopped Jalapeno peppers (You can roast first for a milder flavor)
- 36 oz. cans of tomato paste
- ½ cup of vinegar
- 3 tbsp. of sugar
- 1 tablespoon of salt
- 2 tablespoons of garlic powder
- 3 tablespoons of cayenne pepper (Use less for Milder Heat)
- (Optional) 4 tablespoons of cilantro

Cooking Instructions:

1. Combine all ingredients in your Instant Pot. Select Manual button, adjust time to cook at High Pressure for 30 minutes.

2. After the 30 minutes, allow the cooker to release pressure naturally.

3. Allow to cool. can or freeze in airtight containers.

BBQ Meatballs

Ingredients:
For the Cherry BBQ Sauce:
- 1 tablespoon of ghee
- 1 cup of sweet onion, diced
- 2 garlic cloves (minced)
- 1 cup of (8 oz.) organic tomato sauce
- ¼ cup of apple cider vinegar
- 2 cups of organic frozen dark cherries
- 1 tablespoon of stone ground mustard
- ½ teaspoon of sea salt
- Black pepper (½ tsp.)

For the meatballs:
- 1 pound of ground pork
- 1 egg
- ¼ cup of sweet onion, minced

Cooking Directions:
1. Press the Sauté button on your Instant Pot, then add ghee to pot.

2. Once ghee is melted, add in onions and sauté until translucent. Add garlic and stir until fragrant.

3. Add in remaining Cherry BBQ Sauce ingredients. Select Manual button, adjust time to cook for about 5 minutes.

4. While the BBQ cooks, mix together meatball ingredients in a large bowl. Use a 1 tbsp. cookie scoop to create uniform meatballs.

5. Roll between your palms and set onto a cookie sheet. Creates 16 to 17 meatballs. Place cookie sheet into fridge.

6. After the 5 minutes, do a quick pressure release until the float valve drops. Remove the Lid carefully. Add meatballs to the sauce and spoon the sauce over all the meatballs.

7. Select the Manual function, set to cook for about 5 minutes. When the timer beeps, do a quick pressure release and remove the meatballs.

8. Set pressure cooker to Sauté, and reduce sauce for 10 minutes, stirring occasionally.

9. Serve immediately and enjoy!

BBQ Pulled Pork

Preparation time: 10 minutes
Cooking time: 60 minutes
Overall time: 1 hour 10 minutes

Ingredients:
- ½ cup of soda or apple cider vinegar
- ½ cup of ketchup
- ⅓ cup of brown sugar
- 1 tablespoon of molasses
- 1 tablespoon worcestershire sauce
- 3 tablespoons of cajun or barbecue seasoning of choice
- 5 lb. of pork shoulder
- Coleslaw (we used homemade Dijon Agave Slaw)
- Slider buns, for serving

Cooking Instructions:
1. Combine the soda or vinegar, ketchup, brown sugar, molasses, and worcestershire sauce in a small bowl.

2. Place the pork shoulder directly in your Instant Pot and pour the homemade BBQ sauce overtop to help the seasoning stick.

3. Sprinkle the seasoning on top of the pork shoulder and rub it in, ensuring that you cover it completely to make a nice bark.

4. Secure the Lid in place and make sure vent is sealed. Select Manual button, adjust time to cook at High Pressure for about 60 minutes.

5. After the 60 minutes, allow the pressure cooker to release pressure naturally.

6. Shred the pork with two forks and add additional BBQ sauce if you like.

7. Serve on slider buns with your favorite coleslaw.

8. Serve immediately and enjoy!

CHAPTER 7: SOUPS & STEW RECIPES

Delicious Borscht (Beet Soup)

Preparation time: 15 minutes
Cooking time: 15 minutes
Overall time: 30 minutes
Serves: 3-4 people

Ingredients:
- 1 medium white onion, chopped
- 1 tsp. of salt
- 2 tbsp. of olive oil
- 2 large white potatoes, peeled and diced into small cubes (about 1 lb. / 450 g)
- 1 large carrot, grated (about 4.5 oz./ 125 g)
- 2 medium beets or 3 small ones, grated (7-8 oz. / 200-250 g)
- ¼ medium white cabbage, thinly sliced (12 oz. / 350 g)
- 4 medium cloves of garlic, diced
- 10 to 12 g dried porcini mushrooms
- 3 tbsp. of apple cider vinegar
- 1.5 tbsp. of tomato paste
- 1 cube of beef stock
- 1 cube of vegetable stock
- ½ tsp. of pepper
- 1.25 Litres filtered water (5 cups)
- Fresh parsley and sour cream/yoghurt to serve

Cooking Directions:
1. Switch your Instant Pot to Sauté mode. (it should say High, 30 minutes).

2. Then add in onions and olive oil. Sauté for 2 minutes, until softened.

3. Add potatoes, carrots and beets, and stir through, then add the cabbage, garlic and the remaining ingredients.

4. Stir through and select Keep Warm/Cancel button. Secure the Lid and make sure the vent is sealed.

5. Select Manual button, adjust timer to cook at High Pressure for about 10 minutes.

6. After the 10 minutes, allow the pressure cooker to release pressure naturally for about 5 minutes before doing a quick pressure release.

7. Serve the soup with chopped fresh parsley and a dollop of sour cream or full-fat Greek yogurt. Serve and enjoy!

Saffron Halibut Stew

Preparation time: 12 minutes
Cooking time: 10 minutes
Overall time: 22 minutes

Ingredients:
- 14.5 oz./1 can chicken broth
- ¼ cup of dry white wine
- red potatoes (use 4 pieces, cut into 4 pieces)
- 3 pieces of carrots, cut into ½- inch chunks)
- onion (1 piece, to be finely chopped)
- 1 bay leaf
- 2 tbsp. of minced
- ¼ cup of chopped parsley Pinch of saffron threads
- 1 lb. of firm halibut (cut into 8 pieces)
- 1 small red pepper (cut into chunks)
- Frozen peas (use 1 cup, thawed)

Cooking Directions:
1. Add in the first 9 Cooking Ingredients into the instant pot. Secure the Lid and make sure vent is closed.

2. Select Manual button, adjust time to cook 5 minutes. After the 5 minutes,

3. Do a quick pressure release until the float valve drops. remove the Lid and add the remaining 3 Cooking Ingredients.

4. Secure the Lid again. Select Manual button, set to cook at High Pressure for 5 minutes.

5. When the time is up, do a quick pressure release.

6. Discard the bay leaf and serve!

Pot Beef Stew

Preparation time: 5 minutes
Cooking time: 60 minutes
overall time: 1 hour 5 minutes
Serves: 6-7 people

Ingredients:

- 2 lb. beef stew meat, (cut into bite-sized pieces)
- 1 tsp. of salt
- 1 tsp. of pepper
- 1 medium onion, finely chopped
- 2 to 3 cloves of garlic, minced
- 6 oz. can tomato paste
- 32 oz. beef broth
- 2 tbsp. of Worcestershire sauce
- 2 cups of baby carrots
- 4 to 5 small red potatoes, cut into bite-sized pieces (about 3 cups)
- 1 tbsp. of dried parsley
- 1 tsp. of oregano
- 1 cups of frozen peas
- 1 cup of frozen corn
- Flour (¼ cup)
- Water (¼ cup)

Cooking Directions:

1. Add all ingredients into the Instant Pot (exception the frozen peas, corn and flour/water mixture).

2. Stir everything together until it is well combined. Secure the Lid in place and make sure vent is sealed.

3. Select Meat/Stew button. When the time is up, allow the cooker to release pressure naturally for about 12 minutes.

4. Do a quick pressure release until the float valve drops. Stir in the frozen corn, peas and flour/water mixture.

5. Stir it very well until the stew thickens a little bit more and the corn/peas are warmed, for about 3 to 5 minutes.

6. Serve immediately and enjoy!

Cuban Shredded Beef Stew

Preparation time: 20 minutes
Cooking time: 40 minutes
Overall time: 1 hour
Serves: 6-7 people

Ingredients:

- 1 tbsp. of olive oil
- 2 lb. of beef flank steak
- Salt & pepper to taste
- 1 medium onion, sliced
- 4 to 5 cloves of garlic, minced
- 1 cup of beef or chicken broth
- one 15 oz. can dice tomatoes
- 2 cups of sliced mild/sweet peppers
- ½ tsp. of dried oregano
- 1 tsp. of ground cumin
- 1 bay leaf
- ½ to 1 tsp. of Goya Saxon or Adobo seasoning
- ½ cup of chopped fresh parsley
- 2 tbsp. of vinegar
- ½ cup of chopped green olives

Cooking Directions:

1. Generously season the flank steak on both sides with salt and pepper. Add the olive oil to the Instant Pot and cook over medium heat.

2. Select the Sauté button to begin cooking at medium heat. Once the oil is hot.

3. Place the meat into the Instant Pot. Ensure that a large flat surface is in contact with the bottom of the pot.

4. brown the meat very well on both sides, and then, transfer it to a plate to rest.

5. Add the onions and garlic to the pot, and keep on cooking over medium Sauté, stirring frequently, until the onions begin to soften.

6. Add the broth and deglaze. Scrape any browned bits from the bottom of the pot. Add the canned tomatoes, sliced peppers, oregano, cumin, and bay leaf and seasoning blend.

7. Give everything a good stir to combine, then nestle the browned flank steak into the stew.

8. Secure the Lid in place and ensure that the steam valve is on sealing position. Set to cook Under High Pressure for 40 minutes.

9. After the 40 minutes, allow the cooker to release pressure naturally for 10 minutes. Then do a quick pressure release until the float valve drops.

10. Remove the Lid and shred the meat by pulling it apart into long fibers with two forks.

11. Discard the bay leaf, and mix in the parsley, vinegar and green olives. Season it to taste and allow it to cool.

12. Serve with rice and enjoy!

Chicken Pot Pie Stew

Preparation time: 10 minutes
Cooking time: 45 minutes
Overall time: 55 minutes
Serves: 6-7 people

Ingredients:

- 4 large frozen chicken breasts
- 1 large onion, chopped
- 1 bag of frozen mixed vegetables
- Sea salt and pepper
- 4 cups of chicken broth
- 1 cup of heavy cream (or milk)
- 2 tbsp. of flour

Cooking Directions:

1. Put the large frozen chicken breasts, chopped onion, salt and pepper into your Instant Pot.

2. Add 4 cups of the chicken broth. Secure the Lid in place and ensure that the steam valve is on sealing position.

3. Select the Soup/Stew function and adjust the timer to cook for about 30 minutes.

4. After the 30 minutes, do a quick pressure release until float valve drops. Open the Lid carefully and remove the chicken breasts to a plate.

5. Allow it to cool for about 5 minutes. Cut the chicken breasts into bite sized pieces and return to the pot.

6. Switch to the Sauté mode so the broth will start boiling. Add the bag of frozen veggies and more broth and allow the mixture to come back up to a boil.

7. In a small mixing bowl, mix the 1 cup of heavy cream with the flour and pour this into the mix to help thicken the soup.

8. Taste and add more seasonings to your desired taste

9. Serve immediately and enjoy!

Peanut Stew

Preparation time: 8 minutes
Cooking time: 10 minutes
Overall time: 18 minutes

Ingredients:

- 1 cup of chopped onion
- 2 tbsp. of minced garlic
- 1 tbsp. of ginger
- 1 tsp. of salt
- ½ tsp. of ground cumin
- ½ tsp. of ground coriander
- ½ tsp. of ground black pepper
- ½ tsp. of ground cinnamon
- 1/8 tsp. of ground cloves
- 1 tbsp. of tomato paste
- 1 lb. of boneless skinless chicken breast or thigh pieces
- 3 to 4 cups of chopped swiss chard
- 1 cup of frozen mixed vegetables
- Water
- ½ cup of chunky peanut butter

Cooking Instructions:

1. Add all the recipe ingredients into the pot (except peanut butter).

2. Select Manual button, adjust timer to cook at High Pressure for 10 minutes.

3. After the 10 minutes, allow the pressure cooker to release pressure naturally.

4. Open the Lid carefully and stir in the peanut butter and taste as you go.

5. Serve when you like the taste.

Beef & Chorizo Stew

Preparation time: 15 minutes
Cooking time: 14 minutes
Overall time: 29 minutes

Ingredients:

- ½ lb. of beef chuck roast (cut into 1½ inch pieces)
- 2 chorizo links
- 1 tsp. of olive oil
- ½ onion (to be finely chopped)
- 1 medium carrot (to be mildly chopped)
- 1 celery stalk (to be chopped)
- 1 green pepper (remove the seeds and dice)
- ½ cup of mushrooms (thinly sliced)
- 2 cloves of garlic (to be minced)
- ½ cup of dry red wine
- 1 tbsp. of tomato paste
- 1 bay leaf
- ½ cup of beef broth
- Salt & pepper to taste

Cooking Directions:

1. Season the beef with pinches of salt and pepper in a separate bowl.

2. Spray a skillet pan with cooking spray and set your gas cooker to medium heat and cook the chorizo in it until soft. When cooked, cut into ½ slices.

3. Preheat the Instant Pot, put olive oil in it. Once the oil gets hot, add the beef pieces and Sauté until lightly browned.

4. After sautéing, set aside the beef to cool and put the onions in the oil for about 2 minutes before adding the carrots, peppers, celery and sauté for 3 minutes.

5. Add garlic and cook-stir for another one minute. Add the red wine into the pot.

6. At this point, cook until wine is reduced by half then pour in the tomato paste, beef, chorizo, bay leaf.

7. Secure the Lid in place and make sure the vent is sealed. Select Manual button, adjust timer to cook for 10 minutes.

8. After the 10 minutes, do a quick pressure release until float valve drops, Add up the mushrooms to pot.

9. Secure the Lid in place and ensure that the steam valve is sealed. Select Manual button, adjust timer to cook at High Pressure for 4 minutes.

10. When the time is up, turn off the pot.

11. Serve garnished with parsley and enjoy!

Pork and Hominy Stew

Recipe Ingredients:
- 2 tbsp. of vegetable oil
- Salt
- 1¼ lb. of boneless pork shoulder (cut and diced into 4-inch)
- 1 medium white onion (to be chopped)
- 4 cloves of garlic (to be minced)
- 2 tbsp. of chili powder
- 4 cups of chicken broth
- 2 cans /29 oz. of hominy to be drained and rinsed
- Diced avocado and lime wedges
- 2 tbsp. of Corn-starch
- ¼ of cold water

Cooking Directions:
1. Switch your Instant Pot to Sauté mode and preheat the Instant Pot.

2. Add oil into the Instant Pot. When hot place in the pork, add some salt to taste and sauté until brown.

3. After sautéing, reserve aside in a different bowl. Add 1 tbsp. of oil into the Instant Pot.

4. Add the onion and sauté until tender, add garlic, and chili powder in it and stir until soft.

5. Add 2 cups of chicken broth into the pot. Use a wooden spoon to scrape up all browning remaining bit.

6. Add the boneless pork should and 2 cups of broth into the pot. Use the soup button to cook the pork.

7. When the time is up, allow the cooker to release pressure naturally for about 10 minutes before doing a quick pressure release.

8. Remove the Lid. Remove the pork, wait to cool for some minutes, shred into pieces, and set aside.

9. While you keep the pork to cool before shredding, quickly whisk the cornstarch with a small amount of cold water in a small bowl.

10. Add broth in the cooking pot. Select Sauté and stir until broth thickens and pour in the shredded pork. Taste and season with salt and pepper if needed.

11. serve with the avocado and lime.

Alphabet Soup

Preparation time: 10 minutes
Cooking time: 15 minutes
Overall time: 25 minutes
Ingredients:

- canned tomatoes (128 oz.)
- 1½ tbsp. of beef base or 5 teaspoons of beef bouillon
- 2 teaspoons of dried onion
- 1 tsp. of granulated garlic
- Carrots, use 3 pieces, to be diced
- ½ cup of uncooked barley / brown rice
- water (use 4 cups/1 Quart)
- green beans (use 1 can)
- Corn (use 1 can)
- alphabet paste (use ½ Cup)

Cooking Directions:

1. Place all other ingredients into your pot (Except the paste, corn, and green beans)
2. Secure the Lid in place and make sure vent is sealed. Select Manual button, adjust the timer to cook on High Pressure for 12 minutes.

3. After the 12 minutes, do a quick pressure release until the float valve drops. Remove the Lid carefully.

4. Add the rest of the ingredients and Secure the Lid. Select Manual button, set to cook at High Pressure for about 3 minutes.

5. After 3 minutes, do a quick pressure release and remove the Lid carefully. add some salt and pepper to taste if you like.

6. Serve immediately and enjoy!

5 Minute Vegetable Soup

Ingredients:
- 1 cup of diced carrots
- ½ cup of diced onions
- 1 stalk celery chopped
- 1 clove garlic chopped
- 1 tbsp. of flour
- 2 cups of stewed tomatoes
- ½ cup of tomato puree
- 3 beef bouillon cubes
- 1.2 Litres of water
- 1 cup cleaned and cut up fresh -string beans
- 1 tbsp. barley
- 1 pinch dried basil
- 1 tbsp. Worcestershire sauce

Cooking Directions:
1. Spray the Instant Pot with Pam, and sauté the carrots, onions, and celery till limp in it.

2. Dust with flour and add all remaining Ingredients. Then secure the Lid.

3. Select the Manual function, set to cook at High Pressure for about 5 minutes.

4. When done, turn off the instant pot. Allow the cooker to release pressure naturally for few minutes before removing the Lid.

5. Serve and enjoy.

Lentil Orzo Soup

Preparation time: 10 minutes
Cooking time: 10 minutes
Total time: 20 minutes
Servings: 8 to 9 people

Recipe Ingredients:

- 1 tbsp. of vegetable oil
- 1 onion, diced
- 3 carrots, diced
- 5 cloves garlic, minced
- 2 cans (15 oz..) diced tomatoes
- 4 cups of chicken broth
- 4 cups of water
- 1 ½ cups brown lentils, rinsed
- 2 tsp of cumin
- 1 tsp garlic salt
- ¼ tsp of red pepper flakes
- 2 tbsp. dried parsley
- ½ tsp. of salt & ½ tsp pepper
- ½ cup of orzo
- 2 cups of roughly chopped baby spinach

Cooking Instructions:

1. Select sauté and add oil to the Instant pot. When the display says hot, sauté onion and carrots in oil until tender (about 8 minutes).

2. Add garlic and cook for one more minute before adding the next 10 Ingredients (tomatoes-pepper).

3. Lock the Lid. Select the Manual function, set to cook at High Pressure for about 10 minutes.

4. When done, do a Quick Pressure Release and remove the Lid carefully. Add the orzo and simmer uncovered for 10 minutes or until orzo and lentils are tender.

5. (to simmer on Instant Pot, select the sauté button and press the adjust button twice to lessen the heat).

6. Add spinach and cook until it wilts before seasoning to taste with additional salt and pepper if needed.

Chilled Fruit Soup

Preparation time: 10 minutes
Cooking time: 5 minutes
Total time: 15 minutes
Serves: 3 to 4 people

Recipe Ingredients:
- ½ cantaloupe (rind removed, cut into large chunks)
- 1 large orange (peeled & halved)
- 2 peaches (pit removed)
- 16 oz. pineapple juice
- 8 oz. plain Greek yogurt
- ½ tsp vanilla
- 1 tbsp. powdered sugar
- 1 tbsp. chia seeds

Cooking Instructions:
1. Add the prepared fruit and pineapple juice to the instant pot pressure cooker and lock the Lid.

2. Select the Manual function, set to cook at High Pressure for about 5 minutes.

3. When the time is up, do a quick pressure release and remove the Lid carefully.

4. Pour into blender and puree until completely smooth, then pour through a strainer to remove any bulky pulp.

5. Allow to cool to room temperature then add Greek yogurt, vanilla, and powdered sugar, then whisk to combine.

6. Chill in the refrigerator and serve cold swirled with extra yogurt and sprinkled with chia seeds.

Creamy Taco Soup

Cooking time: 20 minutes
Preparation time: 10 minutes
Total time: 30 minutes
Serves: 5 to 6

Recipe Ingredients:

Soup:

- 1 ½ tbsp. of ghee or coconut oil
- 1 large yellow onion diced
- 4 bell peppers diced
- 2 lb. of grass-fed ground beef
- 2 to 3 tbsp. of chili powder depending on how spicy you want it
- 2 tbsp. of cumin
- 2 tsp. of sea salt
- 2 tsp. of black pepper
- 1 tsp. of paprika
- 1 tsp. of cinnamon
- ½ tsp. of garlic powder
- ½ tsp. of onion powder
- 1/8 - ¼ tsp. of cayenne pepper depending on how spicy you want it
- 28 oz. of diced tomatoes
- 24 oz. bone broth- Find Here!
- 5 oz. culinary coconut milk
- 8 oz. diced green chiles

Toppings:

- jalapenos
- green onions
- avocado
- cilantro
- lime

Cooking Instructions:

1. Switch your Instant Pot to Sauté mode and melt the ghee in your Instant Pot.

2. Add the onions and bell peppers and Sauté until soft and tender. This will take 5 to 7 minutes.

3. Add the grassfed ground beef and stir until is cooked through and no longer pink.

4. Drain the beef through a colander and re-add it to the Instant Pot. Add all of the spices and give everything a good stir.

5. Add diced tomatoes, broth, coconut milk and green chiles and stir until well combined.

6. Secure the Lid and make sure the vent is closed. Press the Soup button and press the "-" button to change the cooking time to 25 minutes.

7. When the time is up, do a quick pressure release. Remove the Lid and add any or all of the toppings listed.

8. Serve and enjoy.

Buffalo Chicken Soup

Preparation time: 10 minutes
Cooking time: 10 minutes
Total time: 20 minutes
Serves: 2 to 3 people

Recipe Ingredients:

- 2 boneless skinless chicken breasts, frozen is ok, no need to thaw.
- 3 cups of chicken bone broth
- ½ cup of diced celery
- ¼ cup of diced onion
- 1 clove garlic, chopped
- 1 tbsp. my Homemade ranch dressing mix
- 2 tbsp. of ghee or butter
- 1/3 cup of hot sauce
- 2 cups of cheddar cheese, shredded
- 1 cup of organic heavy cream

Cooking Instructions:

1. Combine all ingredients in your Pressure Cooker (Except cream & cheese).

2. Select the Manual function, set to cook under pressure for 10 about minutes

3. When the time is up, do a quick pressure release. Remove the Lid carefully, shred and return to soup.

4. Add heavy cream and cheese, give everything a good stir to combine.

5. Serve and enjoy.

Chorizo Corn Chowder

Recipe Ingredients:

- 3 tbsp. of butter
- 1 large yellow onion (diced)
- ½ tsp. of salt
- ½ tsp. of pepper
- 2 ½ tsp. of dried thyme
- 1 lb. of chorizo
- 3 tbsp. of flour
- 2 15.25oz cans corn (I used organic sweet corn)
- 4 cups of chicken stock
- 4 potatoes (diced)
- 1 cup of heavy whipping cream

Cooking Instructions:

1. Switch your Instant Pot to Sauté mode and melt butter. Sauté onions until translucent.

2. Add in salt, pepper, thyme, and chorizo. Cook approximately 5 minutes until meat begins to brown.

3. Turn off the Instant Pot sauté heat. Add ½ can of corn directly into the Instant Pot.

4. In a blender, add the remaining 1½ cans of corn and 1½ cups of chicken stock and blend to a coarse chop.

5. Add the blended corn and chicken stock mixture into your Instant Pot. Then add in remaining chicken stock, potatoes, and cream.

6. Select the Manual function, set to cook at High Pressure for about 12 minutes.

7. When the time is up, allow the cooker to release pressure naturally for about 5 minutes. Then do a quick pressure release. Open the Lid carefully.

8. Serve and enjoy.

Chunky Beef, Cabbage and Tomato Soup

Total time: 40 minutes
Preparation time: 10 minutes
Cooking time: 30 minutes

Recipe Ingredients:

- 1 lb. of 90% lean ground beef
- 1-½ teaspoon kosher salt
- ½ cup of diced onion
- ½ cup of diced celery
- ½ cup of diced carrot
- 28 oz. can diced or crushed tomatoes
- 5 cups of chopped green cabbage
- 4 cups of beef stock (canned or homemade)
- 2 bay leaves

Cooking Instructions:

1. Select the Sauté function on your Instant Pot, let the Instant Pot get very hot, when hot spray with oil, add the ground beef and salt.

2. Cook until browned breaking the meat up into small pieces as it cooks, cook for about 3 to 4 minutes.

3. When browned, add the onion, celery and carrots and Sauté for about 4 to 5 minutes.

4. Add the tomatoes, cabbage, beef stock and bay leaves. Secure the Lid and make sure the vent is closed.

5. Select the Manual function, set to cook at High Pressure for about 20 minutes.

6. When the time is up, allow the cooker to release pressure naturally. Remove bay leaves and serve. Makes 11 cups.

Stuffed Pepper Soup

Total time: 45 minutes
Preparation time: 10 minutes
Cooking time: 35 minutes

Recipe Ingredients:

- 3 cups of cooked brown rice (omit for paleo diet)
- 1 pound of 95% lean ground beef
- ½ cup of chopped green bell pepper
- ½ cup of chopped red bell pepper
- 1 cup of finely diced onion
- 3 cloves garlic, chopped
- 2 cans (14.5 oz. each) cans petite diced tomatoes
- 1 ¾ cups of tomato sauce
- 2 cups of reduced sodium, fat-free chicken broth
- ½ teaspoon of dried marjoram
- Salt and fresh pepper to taste

Cooking Instructions:

1. Select the Sauté function on your Instant Pot, spray the pot with nonstick spray, add the ground meat and salt.

2. Cook until no longer pink, for about 5 to 8 minutes. Drain fat if any, then add peppers, onions and garlic and cook for about 4 to 5 minutes.

3. Add tomatoes, tomato sauce, chicken broth, marjoram and season with salt and pepper to taste.

4. Secure the Lid and make sure the vent is closed. Select the Manual function, set to cook at High Pressure for about 15 minutes.

5. When the time is up, allow the cooker to release pressure naturally. Serve about 1 ½ cups of soup in each bowl and top with ½ cup of cooked brown rice.

6. Serve and enjoy.

Cheeseburger Soup

Total time: 30 minutes
Preparation time: 10 minutes
Cooking time: 20 minutes

Recipe Ingredients:
- ½ lb. fit & active 93% lean ground turkey
- 1 tbsp. of unsalted butter
- 1 medium onion, chopped
- 2 medium carrots, chopped
- 2 celery stalks, chopped
- 2 garlic cloves, minced
- 2 tbsp. all-purpose flour
- ½ tsp. of kosher salt
- Freshly ground black pepper
- 3½ cups of simply nature organic low sodium free range chicken broth
- 10 oz. Yukon gold potatoes (2 medium), peeled and finely diced
- 1 (12-oz.) wedge cauliflower (1/4 of a large head), stem attached
- 1¾ cups of shredded fit & active 2% milk sharp cheddar cheese
- 2 tbsp. of chopped scallions, for garnish

Cooking Instructions:
1. Select the Sauté function on your Pressure Cooker. Add the turkey and brown the meat.

2. Use a wooden spoon to break it into small pieces as it cooks, for about 4 to 5 minutes.

3. Drain the meat and transfer it to a small bowl. In the pressure cooker (still on sauté), melt the butter. Add in the onion, carrots, celery, and garlic.

4. Cook, stirring, until softened, for about 5 minutes. Then add the flour, salt, and pepper to taste.

5. Cook, stirring, for 1 minute to cook the flour. Return the turkey to the pressure cooker.

6. Add the chicken broth, potatoes, and cauliflower, give everything a good stir.

7. Secure the Lid and make sure the vent is closed. Select the Manual function, set to cook at High Pressure for about 10 minutes, until the potatoes are soft.

8. When the time is up, do a quick pressure release. Then open the Lid carefully.

9. Transfer the cauliflower and 1 cup of the liquid to a blender. Blend until smooth.

10. Pour the puree into the soup and give everything a good stir.

11. Add the cheddar and stir until melted.

12. Serve topped with the scallions. Serve and enjoy.

Beef, Tomato and Acini Di Pepe Soup

Total time: 45 minutes
Preparation time: 10 minutes
Cooking time: 35 minutes
Recipe Ingredients:
- 1 pound of 90% lean ground beef
- ½ tsp. of kosher salt
- ½ cup of diced onion
- ½ cup of diced celery
- ½ cup of diced carrot
- 28 oz. can diced tomatoes
- 32 oz. beef stock*
- 2 bay leaves
- 4 oz. small pasta such as Acini di pepei*
- grated parmesan cheese, optional

Cooking Instructions:
1. Select the Sauté function, when it's very hot, add the ground beef and salt, cook until browned.

2. Use a wooden spoon to break up the meat into small pieces as it cooks. When browned, add the onion, celery and carrots and Sauté for about 3 to 4 minutes.

3. Add the tomatoes, beef stock and bay leaves. Secure the Lid and make sure the valve is closed.

4. Select the Soup function, set to cook for 35 minutes. When the time is up, do a quick pressure release.

5. Remove the Lid, add pasta and stir. Select the Manual function, set to cook at High Pressure for about 6 minutes.

6. Remove bay leaves, serve and enjoy.

Creamy Chicken Noodle Soup

Preparation time: 10 minutes
Cooking time: 10 minutes
Total time: 30 minutes
Serves: 3 to 4 people

Recipe Ingredients:

- 3 large carrots peeled and sliced (not too thin)
- 2 ribs celery sliced
- 1 cup of chopped spinach
- 1 boneless skinless chicken breast chopped (fresh or frozen)
- 1 tsp. of parsley
- 1 tsp. of salt
- ½ tsp. of thyme
- ¼ tsp. of garlic powder
- 1/8 tsp. of black pepper
- 4 cups of low sodium chicken broth
- 1 cup of short pasta such as Ditalini or Orzo
- 1 cup 1% milk
- 2 tbsp. of corn starch

Cooking Instructions:

1. Add carrots, celery, spinach, chicken, parsley, salt, thyme, garlic powder, black pepper and chicken broth to your Instant Pot. Give everything a good stir.

2. Secure the Lid and make sure vent is closed. Select the Manual function, set to cook at High Pressure for about 5 minutes.

3. When the time is up, do a quick pressure release and remove the Lid carefully.

4. Switch your Instant Pot to Sauté mode and add the pasta. Cook and stir for 4 to 5 minutes until pasta is al dente.

5. Whisk together the milk and corn starch and stir into the soup. It will thicken immediately and continue to thicken as it sits and cools.

6. Serve and enjoy.

CHAPTER 8: DESSERT RECIPES

Easy Smooth Flan (Crème Caramel)

Preparation time: 25 minutes
Cooking time: 25 minutes
Total time: 50 minutes
Serves: 5 to 6 people
Recipe Ingredients:
Caramel:
- ½ cup of (100 g) white sugar
- 2 tbsp. of (30 ml) water

Flan:
- 1 cup of (250 ml) 2% milk
- 1 cup of (250 ml) heavy cream
- ¼ cup of (50 g) sugar
- 2 tsp. of (10 ml) vanilla extract
- 1 pinch of sea salt
- 3 extra large eggs, lightly beaten

Cooking Instructions:
1. Make Caramel: Heat sugar and water in a saucepan over medium high heat. Swirl occasionally until dark golden brown (mahogany) in color.

2. Divide the caramel into six 177 ml ramekins and allow the caramel to cool.

3. Heat up the milk and heavy cream in a medium pot. Then add in sugar, vanilla extract, and sea salt to the hot milk and stir until the sugar has fully dissolved.

4. Beat the eggs lightly in a medium bowl, slowly bring the eggs temperature up by pouring a little warm milk mixture into the eggs at a time.

5. Continue to whisk and pour the remaining milk mixture into the eggs. Pour the mixture into the caramel-filled ramekins through a strainer.

6. Use a spoon to remove all the bubbles on the surface. Cover each ramekin tightly with aluminum foil.

7. Add ½ cup (125 ml) of water in the pressure cooker. Place trivet in the pressure cooker.

8. Put the covered ramekins on the rack. Select the Manual/Pressure Cook function, set to cook at High Pressure for about 9 minutes.

9. When the time is up, allow the cooker to release pressure naturally. Remove the Lid carefully.

10. Remove ramekins from the pressure cooker. Set aside to cool. Refrigerate to firm for at least 4 hours or overnight.

11. Run a knife around the ramekins and invert onto a plate.

12. Serve and enjoy.

Chocolate Pots De Crème

Recipe Ingredients:
- 1 ½ cups of heavy cream
- ½ cup of whole milk
- 5 large egg yolks
- ¼ cup of sugar
- pinch of salt
- 8 oz. bittersweet chocolate, melted
- whipped cream and grated chocolate for decoration, optional

Cooking Instructions:
1. In a small saucepan, bring the cream and milk to a simmer. Then whisk together egg yolks, sugar, and salt in a large mixing bowl.

2. Whisk in the hot cream and milk. Whisk in chocolate until blended. Pour into 6 custard cups. (We used ½ pint mason jars.)

3. Add in 1½ cups of water to your Pressure Cooker and place the steamer rack in the bottom.

4. Place 3 cups on the steamer rack and place a second steamer rack on top of the cups. Stack the remaining three cups on top of the second steamer rack.

5. Secure the Lid and make sure vent is closed. Select the Manual/Pressure Cook function, set to cook at High Pressure for about 6 minutes.

6. After the 6 minutes, allow the cooker to release pressure for about 15 minutes. Then do a quick pressure release.

7. Remove the Lid carefully and remove the cups to a wire rack to cool uncovered.

8. When cool, refrigerate covered with plastic wrap for at least 4 hours or overnight.

9. Serve cool and enjoy.

Chocolate Mousse

Preparation time: 10 minutes
Cooking time: 20 minutes
Total time: 30 minutes
Serves: 4 to 5 people

Recipe Ingredients:

- 4 egg yolks
- ½ cup of Swerve
- ¼ cup of water
- ¼ cup of cacao
- 1 cup of whipping cream
- ½ cup of almond milk
- ½ tsp. of vanilla
- ¼ tsp. of sea salt

Cooking Instructions:

1. In a medium bowl, Add the yolks and whisk until beaten. In a sauce pan, add the Swerve, water and cacao.

2. whisk until sugar is melted and cacao is well combined. Add the cream and almond milk to the pan and whisk to well combine.

3. Let it heat up but not boil and then turn off heat. Add in the salt and vanilla. Mix well to combine.

4. Pour a tbsp. of the warm chocolate mixture into the bowl with the eggs and whisk to combine.

5. Then pour the chocolate into the bowl while whisking until it's well incorporated. Pour mixture into ramekins or jars.

6. Add in 1½ cups of water into your Instant Pot along with a steamer rack. Place ramekins or jars on steamer rack.

7. Secure the Lid and make sure the vent is closed. Select the Manual function, set to cook for about 6 minutes.

8. When the time is up, do a quick pressure release and take out the jars. They will be very hot so use something to pull them out.

9. Let them cool on the counter and then refrigerate for 4-6 hours or overnight. Serve cool and enjoy.

Egg Custard

Preparation time: 5 minutes
Cooking time: 7 minutes
Total time: 12 minutes
Serves: 5 to 6 people

Recipe Ingredients:
- 4 cups of whole milk or cream
- 6 large Eggs
- ¾ cup of white sugar
- 1 teaspoon pure vanilla extract (optional)
- Tiniest pinch sea salt
- ¼ tsp. ground cinnamon (optional)
- Stainless steel (Rice) pan insert

Garnish:
- Whole nutmeg freshly grated
- Fresh fruit
- Ground cinnamon

Cooking Instructions:
1. In a medium bowl, beat eggs. Add milk, sugar, salt and vanilla and blend until combined.

2. Pour into Pressure Cooker safe bowl and cover with foil, create holes for vent. Add 1.5 cups of water to Pressure Cooker cooking pot and place trivet in bottom.

3. Place bowl on top of steamer rack. Secure the Lid and make sure the vent is closed.

4. Select the Manual/Pressure Cook function, set to cook at High Pressure for about 7 minutes.

5. When the time is up, allow the cooker to release pressure naturally for about 10 minutes.

6. Pour off the little bet of whey that gathers on top and then top with a dusting of nutmeg, berries or other fruit, if you like.

7. Serve and enjoy.

Bhapa Doi (Steamed Yogurt Pudding)

Preparation time: 4 minutes
Cooking time: 13 minutes
Total time: 17 minutes
Serves: 3 to 4 people
Recipe Ingredients:
- 14 oz. sweetened condensed milk
- 1.2-1.5 cups Homemade Greek yogurt cheese full fat
- 1 tsp. of butter for greasing
- 5 6 oz. Ramekins

Add ins:
- 1 tsp. of natural cocoa powder
- 5 crushed green cardamon pods for dusting
- 1 round silicone pan cover

Cooking Instructions:
1. Grease Ramekins well and reserve aside. Then add sweetened condensed milk to a glass (liquid) measuring cup.

2. Add 1.25 cups of yogurt and whisk. Add more Yogurt, if mixture is overly sweet.

3. Grease 5 Ramekins. Fill each Ramekin evenly with the mixture. Add 2 cups of water and a steamer rack to Pressure Cooker cooking pot.

4. Place Ramekins on top of steamer rack. Place a foil over Ramekins, so that water does not get into the Ramekins.

5. Secure the Lid and make sure the vent is closed. Select the Manual/Pressure Cook function, set to cook at High Pressure for about 13 minutes.

6. When the time is up, allow the cooker to release pressure naturally for about 15 minutes. Then do a quick pressure release.

7. Serve warm, or place in the refrigerator for a chilled and dense dessert. Turn out onto a plate, or serve right in the Ramekin.

8. Serve and enjoy.

Crème Brulee

Preparation time: 5 minutes
Cooking time: 15 minutes
Total time: 20 minutes
Serve: 5 to 6

Recipe Ingredients:
- 8 egg yolks
- 1/3 cup of granulated sugar
- Pinch of salt
- 2 cups of heavy cream
- 2 tsp. of vanilla
- 6 tbsp. of sugar (superfine if available)

Cooking Directions:
1. Place the steamer rack in your pressure cooker and pour in 1½ cups of water. In a large mixing bowl, whisk together eggs yolks, 1/3 cup granulated sugar and pinch of salt.

2. Whisk in cream and vanilla. Strain the mixture through a mesh sieve into a large measuring bowl with a pitcher.

3. Divide the mixture evenly between 6 custard cups or small ramekins. Cover ramekins with foil.

4. Place on steamer rack in pressure cooking pot, stacking the cups in two second layer.

5. Secure the Lid and close pressure valve. Select the Manual/Pressure Cook function, set to cook at High Pressure for about 6 minutes.

6. When the time is up, allow the cooker to release pressure naturally for about 10 minutes. Then do a quick pressure release.

7. Open the Lid carefully and remove the cups to a wire rack. Uncover and cool completely.

8. Once cooled, cover with plastic wrap and refrigerate for at least 4 hours or up to 2 days before serving.

9. Sprinkle about a tbsp. of sugar (superfine works best) over the entire surface of each custard.

10. Working with one at a time, move the flame of a kitchen torch 2 inches above the surface of each custard in a circular motion to melt and caramelize the sugar. Serve cool and enjoy.

Rice Pudding

Serves: 5 to 6 people

Recipe Ingredients:

- 2 cups of raw whole milk or dairy-free milk of choice
- 1¼ cups of water
- 1 cup of basmati rice
- ¾ cup of heavy cream or coconut cream
- ¼ cup of maple syrup
- 1/8 tsp. of sea salt
- Inside scrapings from 1 vanilla bean or 1 tsp. of vanilla extract

Cooking Instructions:

1. Place rice in fine mesh colander. Rinse well in several changes of water.

2. Place rice in your Instant Pot. Add in water, milk, maple syrup, and sea salt. Stir briefly.

3. Secure the Lid and make sure the vent is closed. Select the Porridge button. The rice will take 20 minutes to cook on this setting.

4. When the time is up, allow the cooker to release pressure naturally for about 10 minutes. Then do a quick pressure release.

5. Remove the Lid carefully and stir until well mixed. Serve with optional toppings.

6. Serve and enjoy.

Rice Pudding

Apple Comfort

Total time: 42 minutes
Preparation time: 30 minutes
Cooking time: 12 minutes
Makes: 8 servings

Recipe Ingredients:
- 1 cup of water
- 6 medium tart apples, peeled and sliced
- 1 cup of sugar
- ¼ cup of all-purpose flour
- 2 tsp. of ground cinnamon
- 2 large eggs
- 1 cup of heavy whipping cream
- 1 tsp. of vanilla extract
- 1 cup of graham cracker crumbs
- ½ cup of chopped pecans
- ¼ cup of butter, melted
- Vanilla ice cream, optional

Cooking Instructions:
1. Add in 1 cup water to your Pressure Cooker. Combine apples, sugar, flour and cinnamon in a large bowl.

2. Spoon into a greased 1-1/2-qt. souffle or round baking dish. In a small bowl, whisk eggs, cream and vanilla; pour over apple mixture.

3. Combine cracker crumbs, pecans and butter in a medium bowl, sprinkle over top.

4. Loosely cover dish with foil to prevent moisture from getting into the dish. Place on a steamer rack with handles, lower into Pressure Cooker.

5. Secure the Lid in place and make sure vent is closed. Select the Manual function, set to cook at High Pressure for about 12 minutes.

6. When the time is up, allow the cooker to release pressure naturally for about 10 minutes before doing a quick pressure release.

7. Serve warm, with ice cream if desired. Serve and enjoy.

Greek Yogurt

Recipe Ingredients:
- 1-gallon whole milk
- 1/3 cup of yogurt starter Greek yogurt
- 1 tablespoon. of vanilla extract (optional)
- ¼ cup of honey (optional)
- Wire sieve
- Nut milk bag or cheese cloth

Cooking Instructions:
1. Pour gallon milk into your Instant Pot. Secure the Lid and make sure the vent is closed.

2. Select the yogurt button, then press the Adjust button until display reads (boil).

3. The milk will boil for about 1 hour. When the time is up, open lid carefully and remove pot from the base.

4. Stir and let milk cool until it reaches 110 to 115 degrees. we laid a set of tongs over the top of the instant pot to hold up the digital thermometer.

5. Allow the milk to cool for about 1-hour. Whisk in the starter (Greek yogurt). If you want to make vanilla or sweetened yogurt.

6. Mix in the vanilla extract and honey. For plain yogurt omit the vanilla extract and honey.

7. Place pot back into base. Secure the Lid and close the vent. Incubate the yogurt by using the yogurt function.

8. If the yogurt function is still set to (boil) select the adjust button until your display reads "8:00". I had to press the adjust button twice.

9. when the incubation period is up, you will need to strain the whey from the yogurt to make it thick like Greek yogurt.

10. Pour yogurt into another large bowl. Place a wire sieve over the Instant Pot and line it with a nut milk bag.

11. Strain the yogurt for 45 minutes. When it's done, pour the yogurt left in the nut milk bag back into the bowl and give it another whisk to break apart any clumps.

12. Fill your jars with the yogurt and refrigerate overnight before using. To make the parfait or fruit bowl, layer yogurt in a cup with fresh seasonal fruit, honey or jam, and granola.

Molten Mocha Cake

Total time: 35 minutes
Preparation time: 10 minutes
Cooking time: 25 minutes
Makes: 6 servings

Recipe Ingredients:
- 1 cup of water
- 4 large eggs
- 1 to ½ cups of sugar
- ½ cup of butter, melted
- 1 tbsp. of vanilla extract
- 1 cup all-purpose flour
- ½ cup of baking cocoa
- 1 tbsp. of instant coffee granules
- ¼ tsp. of salt
- Fresh raspberries or sliced fresh strawberries and vanilla ice cream, (Optional)

Cooking Instructions:
1. Pour water into a 6-qt. Pressure Cooker. In a medium bowl, beat eggs, sugar, butter and vanilla until blended.

2. In another bowl, whisk flour, cocoa, coffee granules and salt; gradually beat into egg mixture.

3. Then transfer to a greased 1-1/2-qt. baking dish. Cover loosely with foil to prevent moisture from getting into dish.

4. Place on a steamer rack with handles, lower into pressure cooker. Secure the Lid and make sure the valve is on sealing position.

5. Select the Manual function, set to cook at High Pressure for about 25 minutes.

6. When the time is up, allow the cooker to release pressure naturally for about 10 minutes. Then do a quick pressure release.

7. Serve with warm cake, berries and ice cream if you desire.

Cherry & Spice Rice Pudding

Cooking time: 3 minutes
Preparation time: 15 minutes
Total Time: 18 minutes
Makes: 12 servings

Recipe Ingredients:
- 4 cups of cooked rice
- 1 can (12 oz.) evaporated milk
- 1 cup of 2% milk
- 1/3 cup of sugar
- ¼ cup of water
- ¾ cup of dried cherries
- 3 tbsp. of butter, softened
- 2 tsp. of vanilla extract
- ½ tsp. of ground cinnamon
- ¼ tsp. of ground nutmeg

Cooking Instructions:
1. Grease a 6-qt. Pressure Cooker. Add rice, milks, sugar and water, give everything a good stir to combine.

2. Stir in remaining ingredients. Secure the Lid and make sure vent is closed.

3. Select the Manual function, set to cook at High Pressure for about 3 minutes.

4. When the time is up, allow the cooker to release pressure naturally for about 5 minutes. Then do a quick pressure release.

5. Stir lightly. Serve warm or cold. Refrigerate leftovers.

Cherry & Spice Rice Pudding

Maple French Toast

Total time: 30 minutes
Preparation time: 10 minutes
Cooking time: 20 minutes
Makes: 4 servings

Recipe Ingredients:
- 6 cups of cubed bread (about 6 oz.)
- 4 oz. cream cheese, cubed
- 4 large eggs
- ½ cup 2% milk
- ¼ cup of maple syrup
- 1 cup of water
- Additional maple syrup

Cooking Instructions:
1. Arrange half of the bread cubes in a greased 1-1/2-qt. baking dish. Then top with cream cheese and remaining bread.

2. Whisk eggs, milk and syrup in a large mixing bowl, pour over bread. Let stand for about 30 minutes.

3. Pour water into your Pressure Cooker. Cover baking dish with foil, place on a steamer rack with handles, lower into Pressure Cooker.

4. Secure the Lid and make sure vent is closed. Select the Manual function, set to cook at High Pressure for about 20 minutes.

5. When the time is up, allow the cooker to release pressure naturally for about 10 minutes before doing a quick pressure release.

6. Remove the Lid carefully, remove baking dish using handles. Serve with syrup.

7. Serve and enjoy.

Thai Coconut Pandan Custard

Preparation time: 5 minutes
Cooking time: 30 minutes
Total time: 35 minutes
Serves: 3 to 4 people

Recipe Ingredients:
- 1 cup of unsweetened coconut milk
- 3 eggs
- 1/3 cup of Truvia baking blend or another sweetener
- 3 to 4 drops of pandan extract (or sub vanilla extract if you must)

Cooking Instructions:
1. Blend the eggs, milk, sweetener and the pandan extract.

2. Pour it into a 6-inch heatproof bowl. Cover with foil. Then place 2 cups of water into your liner, place a steamer rack in the liner, and place your bowl onto the steamer rack.

3. Select the Manual function, set to cook at High Pressure for about 30 minutes.

4. When the time is up, allow the cooker to release pressure naturally. A knife inserted into the custard should come out clean.

5. Cool in refrigerator until the custard is set. Serve and enjoy.

Keto Almond Carrot Cake

Preparation time: 10 minutes
Cooking time: 50 minutes
Total time: 1 hour
Serves: 7 to 8

Recipe Ingredients:

- 3 eggs
- 1 cup of almond flour
- 2/3 cup Swerve
- 1 tsp. of baking powder
- 1.5 tsp. of apple pie spice
- ¼ cup of coconut oil
- ½ cup of heavy whipping cream
- 1 cup of carrots shredded
- ½ cup of walnuts chopped

Cooking Instructions:

1. Grease a 6-inch cake pan. Mix all the ingredients using a hand mixer, until the mixture is well-incorporated, and looks fluffy.

2. Pour into the greased pan and cover the pan with foil. In the inner liner of your Instant Pot, place two cups of water, and a trivet.

3. Place the foil-covered cake on the steamer rack. Select the Cake function, allow it to cook for about 40 minutes.

4. If you don't have a Cake button. Select the Manual function, set to cook at High Pressure for about 40 minutes.

5. When the time is up, Allow the cooker to release pressure naturally for about 10 minutes. Then do a quick pressure release.

6. Allow it to cool before icing with a frosting of your choice.

7. Serve and enjoy.

CHAPTER 9: FISH & SEAFOODS

Frozen Salmon

Preparation time: 5 minutes
Cooking time: 3 minutes
Total time: 8 minutes
Serves: 2 to 3 people

Recipe Ingredients:
- 1 cup of cold water
- ¼ cup of lemon juice
- Non-stick cooking spray
- Salt and ground black pepper to taste
- 2 frozen salmon fillets

Cooking Instructions:
1. Pour the cold water and lemon juice into the Instant Pot.

2. Place a steamer rack in the bottom of the Instant Pot and spray it with the non-stick cooking spray.

3. Place the frozen salmon fillets on the steamer rack, skin-side down. Secure the Lid and make sure vent is closed.

4. Set the Instant Pot to the Steam setting, cook for about 4 minutes. When the time is up, do a quick pressure release.

5. Check the salmon for your preferred doneness and the fish should easily flake with a fork.

6. Season with salt and pepper to taste. Secure the Lid again to keep the salmon warm until serving.

7. Serve and enjoy.

Fish with Orange & Ginger Sauce

Preparation time: 10 minutes
Cooking time: 7 minutes
Total time: 17 minutes
Serves: 3 to 4 people

Recipe Ingredients:
- 4 white fish fillets
- 1 orange zest and juice
- Thumb sized piece of ginger, chopped
- 4 spring onions
- 2 tbsp. of olive oil
- Salt and pepper
- 1 cup of fish stock or white wine

Cooking Instructions:
1. First, take out the fish fillets and dry them using a paper towel.

2. Generously rub the olive oil onto the fish fillet and season lightly.

3. Add the white fish, spring onions, ginger, orange zest and juice into the Instant Pot.

4. Place the fish into the steamer basket in the bottom of Instant Pot. Secure the Lid and make sure vent is closed.

5. Select the Manual function, set to cook at High Pressure for about 7 minutes.

6. Serve on top of an undressed garden salad.

Teriyaki Jumbo Scallops

Preparation time: 5 minutes
Cooking time: 10 minutes
Total time: 15 minutes
Serves: 3 to 4 people

Recipe Ingredients:
- 1 tbsp. of avocado oil
- 1 lb. of jumbo sea scallops, fresh or thawed from frozen
- ½ cup of coconut amino
- 3 tbsp. of 100% maple syrup
- ½ tsp. of garlic powder
- ½ tsp. of ground ginger
- ½ tsp. of sea salt
- Fresh minced chives, (For garnishing)

Cooking Instructions:
1. Add the 1 tbsp. of avocado oil into the stainless-steel bowl and select the sauté function on your Instant Pot.

2. Sear the scallops for about a few minutes on each side. While the content is cooking on sauté mode.

3. Quickly whisk together the remaining ingredients, leaving the chives out to use in garnishing.

4. Pour your sauce over the scallops. Secure the Lid and make sure vent is closed. Select the Warm/Cancel button.

5. Select the Steam function, Pressure Cook for 10 minutes and allow the scallops to steam.

6. After the 10 minutes, do a quick pressure release. Carefully remove the Lid once it cools.

7. Remove the scallops and set it aside. Serve with minced chives to garnish.

Steamed Alaskan Crab Legs

Preparation time: 5 minutes
Cooking time: 4 minutes
Total time: 9 minutes

Recipe Ingredients:
- 2 to 3 lb. of frozen crab legs
- 1 cup of water
- ½ tbsp. of salt
- Butter, melted for serving

Cooking Instructions:
1. Plug the Instant Pot with the insert set in place. Place a steamer basket into the bottom of the Instant Pot with 1 cup of water and ½ tbsp. of salt.

2. Add half of the frozen crab legs along with 1 tbsp. of salt. Secure the Lid and make sure vent is closed.

3. Select the Manual function, set to cook at High Pressure for about 4 minutes.

4. When the timer beeps, do a quick pressure release. Carefully open the Lid and remove the crab legs.

5. Serve with melted butter.

Fish Fillets & Tomatoes

Preparation time: 5 minutes
Cooking time: 12 minutes
Total time: 17 minutes

Recipe Ingredients:
- 4 white fish fillets
- 1 lb. of cherry tomatoes, halved
- 1 cup of black salt-cured olives (Taggiesche, or French)
- 2 tbsp. of pickled capers
- 1 bunch of fresh thyme
- Olive oil
- 1 clove of garlic, pressed
- Salt and pepper to taste

Cooking Instructions:
1. Place a trivet or steamer basket into the bottom of your Instant Pot.

2. Add 1½ to 2 cups of water and line the bottom of the heat-proof bowl with cherry tomato halves to prevent the fish filet from sticking.

3. Add the thyme and reserve a few springs for garnishing. Place the fish fillets over the cherry tomatoes, and sprinkle with the remaining tomatoes, crushed garlic, a dash of olive oil and a pinch of salt.

4. Insert the dish in the Instant Pot and construct a long aluminum sling to serve as handle.

5. Set the pressure level to low and turn the heat up high. Secure the Lid and make sure the vent is closed.

6. Set low pressure to pressure cook for 8 minutes. When the pan reaches pressure, then, lower the heat.

7. When timer beeps, do a quick pressure release. Place the fish into individual serving plates, and top with the cherry tomatoes.

8. Sprinkle with the olives, capers, fresh thyme, a crackle of pepper and a little swirl of fresh olive oil.

9. Serve and enjoy.

Moules a la Mariniere

Preparation time: 5 minutes
Cooking time: 5 minutes
Total time: 10 minutes

Recipe Ingredients:
- fresh mussels (use 2 lb., make sure it's well washed)
- 1 tbsp. of cooking butter
- 2 tbsp. of chopped onion
- 7 lb. of white wine
- Small bunch of fresh parsley (leaves picked and chopped)

Cooking Instructions:
1. Preheat pressure cooker and add butter to melt and add onions, cook until soft.

2. Then, pour in the wine and wait for the wine to boil. Add the mussels and secure the Lid.

3. Select the Manual function, set to cook for 5 minutes. When the time is up, do a quick pressure release.

4. Open the pot and season with salt and pepper as desired.

5. Dish sprinkled with parsley. Serve and enjoy.

Shrimp Curry

Preparation time: 10 minutes
Cooking time: 6 minutes
Total time: 16 minutes

Recipe ingredients:

- 1½ tbsp. of vegetable oil
- 4 tbsp. of sliced onion
- ¾ teaspoon of cumin seeds
- 2 tsp. of grated fresh turmeric
- 1½ tsp. chili powder
- 1½ tsp. of salt
- tomatoes (4 pieces, to be chopped)
- 2 medium size Yukon gold potatoes (diced)
- 1 tbsp. of fresh lemon juice
- ¼ cup of water
- 1 lb. of medium shrimps (shelled, deveined, remove tail)
- ¾ lb. of large shrimps (shelled, deveined, don't remove the tail)
- 12 sprigs fresh cilantro (for garnish)

Cooking Instructions:

1. Pre-heat instant pot using Sauté button, add oil to heat up.

2. Once the oil gets hot, add up the onions in it and stir for one minute. Add the turmeric, cumin seeds, salt and chili powder.

3. Keep pot open and cook-stir for 2 minutes. Mix in the tomatoes, potatoes, water and lemon juice.

4. Let sit until it starts to boil and add the shrimps. Stir well to coat and then secure the Lid.

5. Select the Manual function, set to cook for about 6 minutes. When the time is up, do a quick pressure release.

6. Open the pot and sprinkle with the cilantro sprigs.

7. Serve and enjoy.

Lobster Tails Under Pressure

Preparation time: 5 minutes
Cooking time: 3 minutes
Total time: 8 minutes

Recipe Ingredients:

- 1 cup water
- Lobster tails ghee (2 lb.)
- Sea salt

Cooking Instructions:

1. Pour 1 cup of water into the Pressure Cooker and put in the steamer basket.

2. Cut lobster tail in half from top to tail after which you place the tail and shell side down, on the steamer basket.

3. Secure the Lid. Select the Manual function, set to cook at High Pressure for about 3 minutes.

4. When the time is up, do a quick pressure release. Open the instant pot, and transfer the lobster tails to a serving dish.

5. serve with melted ghee and enjoy.

Beer Potato Fish

Preparation time: 12 minutes
Cooking time: 40 minutes
Total time: 52 minutes

Recipe Ingredients:
- 2 lb. of fish fillet
- 4 medium size potatoes (peeled and diced)
- 1 cup of beer
- 1 red pepper (sliced)
- 1 tbsp. of oil
- 1 tbsp. of oyster flavored sauce
- 1 tbsp. of rock candy
- 1 tsp. of salt

Cooking Instructions:
1. Place all recipe ingredients into the pot and secure the Lid.

2. Select the chili button set to cook at High Pressure for about 40 minutes.

3. When the time is up, do a quick pressure release.

4. Serve and enjoy.

CHAPTER 10: PREREQUISITES (STOCKS & BROTHS)

Chicken Broth

Total time: 55 minutes
Preparation time: 10 minutes
Cooking time: 45 minutes
Makes: about 5 to 6 cups

Recipe Ingredients:
- 2-1/2 lb. of bony chicken pieces (legs, wings, or back bones)
- 2 celery ribs with leaves, cut into chunks
- 2 medium carrots, cut into chunks
- 2 medium onions, quartered
- 2 bay leaves
- ½ tsp. of dried rosemary, crushed
- ½ tsp. of dried thyme
- 8 to 10 whole peppercorns
- 6 cups of cold water

Cooking Instructions:
1. Add all the ingredients in your Pressure Cooker. Secure the Lid and make sure vent is closed.

2. Select the Manual function, set to cook at High Pressure for about 45 minutes.

3. When the time is up, allow the cooker to release pressure naturally. Remove chicken and set aside until cool enough to handle.

4. Remove meat from bones. Discard bones, save meat for another use. Strain broth, discarding vegetables and seasonings.

5. Refrigerate for about 8 hours or overnight. Skim fat from surface.

Whole30 Beef Bone Broth

Preparation time: 5 minutes

Cooking time: 4 hr. 40 minutes

Total Time 4 hr. 45 minutes

Recipe Ingredients:

- 2 to 3 lb. of beef bones (preferably with marrow)
- 2 bunches Leek Tops (the dark green parts) - rinsed
- 2 medium Carrots - rinsed
- 2 stalks celery - rinsed
- 1 medium red onion (cut in half – rinsed)
- 1 medium Parsnip - rinsed
- 1 head fresh garlic - top trimmed – rinsed
- Fresh ginger root (approximately the size of your thumb – rinsed)
- 1 tablespoon of apple cider vinegar
- (Optional) 3 bay leaves
- 1 small bunch fresh parsley – stems and/or leaves - rinsed
- 1 teaspoon of whole black peppercorns
- 1 tablespoon of kosher salt

Cooking Instructions:

1. Fill half of your Instant Pot with water. Select the Sauté function and bring to a simmer.

2. Add raw beef bones and blanch for about 15 to 20 minutes. Make use a spoon to remove any foam that rises to the surface.

3. Transfer blanched bones to a bowl of cold water or rinse under the faucet and preheat your oven to 450F.

4. Pat blanched bones dry with a paper towel. Then add to a parchment paper-lined sheet pan or roasting tray along with the onion, carrot, parsnip, leek tops, garlic and ginger.

5. Now drizzle everything with a small amount of avocado oil. Transfer to your oven and roast for about 15 to 20 minutes (flip everything halfway).

6. In your empty Instant Pot, add all roasted ingredients, include celery, bay leaves, parsley, apple cider vinegar, salt, and pepper.

7. Fill your Instant Pot with water until the Max line. Secure the Lid and make sure vent is closed.

8. Select the Soup function, set to cook at High Pressure for about 180 to 240 minutes.

9. When the time is up, do a quick pressure release. Set a fine mesh sieve overtop of a pitcher (We used blender canister).

10. Pour broth through sieve and discard everything but the liquid. To store, pour broth into tempered mason jars. Be sure to leave at least 2" of headroom if freezing.

11. Freeze in large, silicon ice molds. Once broth has frozen, transfer ice cubes to a freezer-safe bag for easy storage.

12. Repeat process until all broth has frozen.

Vegetable Broth from Scratch

Preparation time: 10 minutes

Cooking time: 15 minutes

Total time: 25 minutes

Makes: 8 to 9 cups

Recipe Ingredients:

- 1 large onion, quartered
- 2 carrots, halved4-5 stalks of celery, halved (We choose from the leafy portion)
- 2 cobs of corn (corn removed)
- 5 to 6 cloves of garlic, whole3-4" ginger, peeled
- 4 large mushrooms, sliced3 cups (appx.) assorted vegetables/food scraps
- 3 bay leaves
- 10 cups of water
- ¼ teaspoon of turmeric
- ¼ teaspoon of garam masala
- 1 teaspoon of black pepper

Cooking Instructions:

1. Add all the ingredients in your Instant Pot. Secure the Lid and make sure vent is closed.

2. Select the Manual function, set to cook for about 15 minutes. When the time is up, allow it to release pressure naturally.

3. Use immediately, or cool completely and store in jars in the fridge for up to 4 days or freeze.

Shrimp Stock

Preparation time: 5 minutes

Cooking time: 45 minutes

Total time: 50 minutes

Recipe Ingredients:

- 4 cups of water
- Shrimp shells from 2 lb. shrimp
- ½ cup of parsley packed
- 1 celery stick cut into 1-inch slices
- 1 onion quartered
- 2 small bay leaves or 1 large

Cooking Instructions:

1. Add water to your Instant Pot. Add shrimp shells, parsley, celery, onion, bay leaves.

2. Give everything a good stir to combine. Secure the Lid and make sure vent is closed. Select the Manual, set to cook at High Pressure for about 30 minutes.

3. When the time is up, allow the cooker to release pressure naturally. Set a colander in a medium bowl and drain contents of the inner pot into the colander.

4. Transfer the broth to a clean jar and store in the fridge for up to 3 days, until ready to use.

Fish Stock

Preparation time: 10 minutes

Cooking time: 45 minutes

Total time: 55 minutes

Recipe Ingredients:

- 2 large salmon heads cut into quarters
- 2 lemongrass stalks- rough chop
- 1 cup of carrots - rough chop
- 1 cup of celery-rough chop
- 2 garlic cloves peeled
- 4 sprigs of thyme
- 3 teaspoons of vegetable or canola oil Use more as needed

Cooking Instructions:

1. Wash the fish heads in cold water and make sure there is no blood. Pat it dry.

2. Add in oil in a heated pan, lightly sear the fish heads. Cut the vegetables and add to the Pressure Cooker.

3. Add the fish and the thyme sprigs. Then add water that will cover the fish. Secure the Lid and make sure vent is closed.

4. Select the Soup function, set to cook at High Pressure for about 45 minutes.

5. When the time is up, allow the cooker to release pressure naturally for about 15 minutes before doing a quick pressure release. Open the Lid carefully and Strain the vegetables and the fish.

Beef Stock

Preparation time: 10 minutes

Cooking time: 2 hours

Total time: 2 hr. 10 minutes

Recipe Ingredients:

1 lb. of beef bones, or more as desired

1 large sweet onion, unpeeled and cut in half

4 large carrots, cut into 4-inch pieces

4 ribs celery, cut into 4-inch pieces

1 bunch of flat-leaf parsley

4 cloves garlic, halved

1 tbsp. of salt

1 tsp. of whole black peppercorns

1 tsp. of dried thyme

2 bay leaves

6 quarts water, or as needed

Cooking Instructions:

1. Preheat oven to 425 degrees F (220 degrees C). Place beef bones on large baking sheet.

2. Bake for about 15 minutes. Then add in onion halves to baking sheet, bake for more 45 minutes.

3. Place roasted bones and onion in your Pressure Cooker, add carrot, celery, parsley, garlic, salt, peppercorns, thyme, and bay leaves.

4. Pour water up to the 6-quart mark inside your Pressure Cooker. Secure the Lid and make sure vent is closed.

5. Select the Manual function, set to cook at High Pressure for about 1 hour. When the time is up, do a quick pressure release. open pressure cooker carefully.

Low Carb Bone Broth

Preparation time: 5 minutes

Cooking time: 1 hr.

Total time: 1 hr. 5 minutes

Makes: 10 to 12 cups

Recipe Ingredients:

- 1 cooked chicken carcass (most meat removed) & any drippings
- 1-inch knob of ginger
- 1 small onion, quartered (skin on)
- 1 cup of chopped celery tops
- 2 cloves of garlic
- 2 tablespoons of apple cider vinegar
- 3 to 4 liters of filtered water

Cooking Instructions:

1. Combine all of the solid ingredients in your Instant Pot. Pour in the filtered water up to the 4-liter mark.

2. Secure the Lid and make sure vent is closed. Select the Manual function, set to cook at High Pressure for about 60 minutes.

3. When the time is up, allow the cooker to release pressure naturally for one hour.

4. Strain the solids out into a clean pot. Season the broth with sea salt as desired.

5. Chill for several hours or overnight. Remove the solidified fat from the top of the broth and discard.

6. Portion into containers and store for about 1 week in the fridge, or freeze for up to 2 months.

Ham Bone Broth

Preparation time: 2 minutes

Cooking time: 2 hr.

Total time: 2 hr. 2 minutes

Recipe Ingredients:

- Ham bone (all natural)
- Filtered water
- Sea salt to taste

Cooking Instructions:

1. Place ham bone in your Instant Pot and add filtered water to cover bone.

2. Don't fill pot more than 3/4 full. Secure the Lid and make sure vent is closed.

3. Select the Manual function, set to cook at High Pressure for about 120 minutes.

4. When the time is up, allow the cooker to release pressure naturally. Remove the bone and strain broth to remove any small pieces of bone and junk.

5. (Pick the meat off the bone and eat or save for another recipe). Cover the broth and refrigerate to solidify the fat.

6. When fat is hard, remove it and discard. Taste broth and season with salt if desired.

Turkey Stock

Preparation time: 5 minutes

Cooking time: 1 hour 30 minutes

Total time: 1 hour 35 minutes

Serves: 8 cups stock

Recipe Ingredients:

- Use the leftover turkey bones from Thanksgiving dinner
- 1 cup of onion large dice
- 1 cup of celery cut into
- 3-inch pieces
- 1 cup of carrots cut into 3-inch pieces
- 2 cloves garlic leftover turkey carcass
- 8 to 10 cups of water

Cooking Instructions:

1. In your Instant Pot, add in the onion, celery, carrots, garlic and the leftover turkey carcass.

2. Add enough water to hit the 10 cups line in your Instant Pot. Secure the Lid and make sure vent is closed.

3. Select the Manual function, set to cook at High Pressure for about 60 minutes.

4. When the time is up, allow the cooker to release pressure naturally for about 20 to 30 minutes. Then remove the Lid carefully.

5. Pour the stock through a fine mesh strainer. Allow the stock to cool, then transfer to mason jars or plastic containers for storage.

6. Store in the refrigerator for 3 days or in the freezer for up to 4 months.

CHAPTER 11: BEANS AND GRAINS RECIPES

Black Bean Chicken Nachos

Total time: 18 minutes

Preparation time: 10 minutes

Cooking time: 8 minutes

Serves: 6 to 8 people

Recipe Ingredients:

- 1-1/2 lb. of boneless skinless chicken breasts
- 2 jars (16 oz. each) black bean and corn salsa
- 1 medium green pepper, chopped
- 1 medium sweet red pepper, chopped
- 1 package (12 oz.) tortilla chips
- 2 cups of shredded Mexican cheese blend
- minced fresh cilantro, pickled jalapeno slices and sour cream

Cooking Instructions:

1. Place chicken, salsa and peppers in your Pressure Cooker. Secure the Lid in place and make sure vent is closed.

2. Select the Manual function, set to cook at High Pressure for about 8 minutes.

3. When the time is up, allow the cooker to release pressure naturally for about 7 minutes before doing a quick pressure release.

4. Remove chicken, shred with two forks. Then return to Pressure Cooker. Using a slotted spoon, serve chicken over chips.

5. Sprinkle with cheese if you desire, cilantro. Add toppings of choice.

6. Serve and enjoy.

White Bean Chicken Chili

Total time: 35 minutes

Preparation time: 25 minutes

Cooking time: 10 minutes

Serves: 5 to 6 people

Recipe Ingredients:

- ¾ lb. of boneless skinless chicken breasts, cut into 1-1/4-inch pieces
- ¼ tsp. of salt
- ¼ tsp. of pepper
- 2 tbsp. of olive oil, divided
- 1 medium onion, chopped
- 1 jalapeno pepper, seeded and chopped
- 4 garlic cloves, minced
- 2 tsp. of dried oregano
- 1 tsp. of ground cumin
- 2 cans (15 oz. each) cannellini beans, rinsed and drained, divided
- 2-1/2 cups of chicken broth, divided
- 1-1/2 cups of shredded cheddar cheese
- **Optional toppings:** sliced avocado, quartered cherry tomatoes and chopped fresh cilantro

Cooking Instructions:

1. Toss chicken with salt and pepper. Select the Sauté function on your Pressure cooker and adjust for high heat.

2. Heat 1 tbsp. of olive oil. Add chicken, brown on all sides. Remove chicken. Add the remaining oil to Pressure Cooker.

3. Sauté onion until tender. Add jalapeno, garlic, oregano and cumin. then cook and stir for about 2 minutes.

4. Return chicken to Pressure Cooker. In a medium bowl, mash 1 cup of beans, stir in ½ cup of broth.

5. Stir bean mixture and remaining whole beans and broth into chicken mixture.

6. Secure the Lid in place and make sure vent is closed. Select the Manual function, set to cook at High Pressure for about 10 minutes.

7. When the time is up, do a quick pressure release. Give everything a good stir before serving. Sprinkle with cheese, add toppings if desired. Serve and enjoy.

Hearty Pork & Black Bean Nachos

Total time: 55 minutes

Preparation time: 15 minutes

Cooking time: 40 minutes

Serves: 8 to 9 people

Recipe Ingredients:

- 1 package (4 oz.) beef jerky
- 3 lb. of pork spareribs, cut into 2-rib sections
- 4 cans (15 oz. each) black beans, rinsed and drained
- 1 cup of chopped onion
- 6 bacon strips, cooked and crumbled
- 4 tsp. of minced garlic
- 1 tsp. of crushed red pepper flakes
- 4 cups of beef broth, divided
- Tortilla chips
- **Optional toppings:** shredded cheddar cheese, sour cream, thinly sliced green onions, pickled jalapeno slices and chopped tomatoes

Cooking Instructions:

1. Pulse beef jerky in a food processor until finely ground. Working in batches, place 1-1/2 lb. ribs in your Pressure Cooker.

2. Top with half the jerky, two cans beans, ½ cup of chopped onion, three bacon strips, 2 teaspoons of garlic and ½ tsp. of red pepper flakes.

3. Pour in 2 cups of broth. Secure the Lid in place and make sure vent is closed. Select the Manual function, set to cook at High Pressure for about 40 minutes.

4. When the time is up, allow the cooker to release pressure naturally for about 10 minutes before doing a quick pressure release.

5. Remove from Pressure Cooker, make second batch by adding remaining ingredients to cooker. Repeat previous procedure.

6. Allow it to cool, then remove meat from bones, discard bones. Shred the meat with two forks and return it to the Pressure Cooker.

7. Select the Sauté function and adjust for high heat, heat through. Strain pork mixture; discard juices.

8. Serve with chips and toppings as desired. Serve and enjoy.

BBQ Baked Beans

Total time: 45 minutes

Preparation time: 10 minutes

Cooking time: 35 minutes

Makes: 12 servings

Recipe Ingredients:

- 1 package (16 oz.) dried great northern beans
- 2 smoked ham hocks (about ½ lb. each)
- 2 cups of water
- 1 medium onion, chopped
- 2 tsp. of garlic powder, divided
- 2 tsp. of onion powder, divided
- 1 cup of barbecue sauce
- ¾ cup packed brown sugar
- ½ tsp. of ground nutmeg
- ¼ tsp. of ground cloves
- 2 tsp. of hot pepper sauce, optional

Cooking Instructions:

1. Rinse and sort beans, soak according to package directions. Drain and rinse beans, discarding liquid.

2. In your Pressure Cooker, combine beans, ham hocks, water, onion, 1 tsp. of garlic powder and 1 tsp. of onion powder.

3. Secure the Lid in place and make sure vent is closed. Select the Manual function, set to cook at High Pressure for about 30 minutes.

4. When the time is up, allow the cooker to release pressure naturally for about 10 minutes before doing a quick pressure release.

5. Remove ham hocks, allow it to cool slightly. Cut meat into small cubes, discarding bones, return the meat to the Pressure Cooker.

6. Stir in barbecue sauce, brown sugar, nutmeg, cloves, remaining garlic powder, remaining onion powder and, if desired, pepper sauce.

7. Secure the Lid in place and sure vent is closed. Select the Manual function, set to cook at High Pressure for about 3 minutes.

8. When the time is up, allow the cooker to release pressure naturally for 5 minutes before doing a quick pressure release. Serve and enjoy.

Saffron, Almond Rice Pilaf

Total time: 13 minutes
Preparation time: 10 minutes
Cooking time: 3 minutes
Recipe Ingredients:

- 1 14 oz. can chicken broth
- 1¼ cup of water
- Pinch of saffron threads
- 1 tbsp. of butter
- 1 medium onion (finely chopped)
- 1 celery stalk (finely chopped)
- 2 cups long-grain white rice, rinsed
- ½ tsp. of salt
- ½ cup of sliced almonds (toasted)

Cooking Instructions:

1. Select the Sauté function, heat the juices and water in your Instant Pot, until Hot.

2. Disintegrate saffron into the fluid and mix; fill a bowl, cover and set aside. Select the Sauté function and melt the butter in the Pressure Cooker.

3. Add the onions and celery to it. Cook-blend until the point when the vegetables are delicate for 5 minutes or less.

4. Stir in the rice and cook, blending habitually until the point when rice ends up noticeably hazy, ought to do in 1 to 2 minutes.

5. Add saffron soup and salt to the cooker, secure the Lid and make sure vent is closed.

6. Select the Manual function, set to cook at High Pressure for about 3 minutes.

7. When the time is up, allow the cooker to release pressure naturally for about 5 minutes before doing a quick pressure release.

8. Serve and enjoy.

IP Fried Rice

Preparation time: 5 minutes
Cooking time: 6 minutes
Total time: 11 minutes
Serves: 3 to 4 people

Recipe Ingredients:

- 2 cups of long grain rice, uncooked
- 2½ cups of vegetable broth
- 2 carrots, chopped
- 3 tbsp. of extra virgin olive oil
- ½ cup of frozen peas
- 2 medium eggs
- Salt & pepper to taste

Cooking Instructions:

1. Add rice and vegetable stock in the Instant Pot. Mix so the rice is spread around evenly.

2. Add in diced carrots, secure the Lid and make sure vent is sealed. Select the Manual function and set to cook for about 3 minutes.

3. When the time is up, do a quick pressure release. Now mix the rice, it will be quite sticky but it should change its texture and lose quite a lot of its stickiness.

4. Move the rice to a side and select the Sauté function. Add in oil and frozen peas and Sauté for about a minute before mixing everything together.

5. create a well in the middle of the rice and add beaten eggs. Stir the egg into rice and fry everything together for a further 1 to 2 minutes.

6. Taste and season with salt and pepper if necessary.

7. Serve and enjoy.

Steamed Lentils

Preparation time: 10 minutes
Cooking time: 13 minutes
Total time: 23 minutes

Recipe Ingredients:
- 1 tbsp. of extra virgin olive oil
- 1 medium onion (chopped)
- 1 stalk celery (chopped)
- 1 medium green pepper (use red pepper if you want)
- 1½ cups of chopped tomatoes
- 1 tsp. of salt
- A few grinds black pepper
- 1 tsp. of curry powder (optional)
- 1½ cups of dry lentils
- 2 cups (500ml) of water

Cooking Instructions:
1. Select the Sauté function and preheat the Instant Pot, add olive oil to it.

2. Sauté the onion, celery, and pepper in it for few minutes, then add in the slashed tomatoes.

3. Mix and sprinkle with salt, pepper, and curry (if using). Add the lentils, some water and blend for a long time.

4. Secure the Lid and make sure vent is closed. Select the Manual function, set to cook at High Pressure for about 13 minutes.

5. When the time is up, allow the cooker to release pressure naturally for 10 minutes before doing a quick pressure release.

6. Remove the Lid carefully and serve.

Lemon Rice

Preparation time: 5 minutes
Cooking time: 4 minutes
Total time: 9 minutes
Serves: 5 to 6 people

Recipe Ingredients:
- 2 tbsp. of butter
- 2 cups of long grain rice
- 1 can (14.5 oz.) chicken broth
- 1 cup of water
- ¼ cup of lemon juice 1 tsp salt
- Fresh parsley (chopped optional)

Cooking Instructions:
1. Select the Sauté function on your Instant Pot and melt the butter in the Instant Pot. Add in the rice.

2. Cook-mix until the point when the rice winds up plainly misty (for about 1 to 2 minutes).

3. Add in the soup, water, lemon squeeze, and salt. Secure the Lid and make sure vent is closed.

4. Select the Manual function, set to cook at High Pressure for about 4 minutes.

5. When the time is up, allow the cooker to release pressure naturally for about 5 minutes before doing a quick pressure release.

6. Fluff rice with a fork and serve decorated with slashed crisp parsley (optional). fluff rice, blend in almonds.

7. Serve and enjoy.

Butternut, Chard & White Bean Soup

Preparation time: 12 minutes
Cooking time: 45 minutes
Total time: 57 minutes
Serves: 5 to 6 people
Recipe Ingredients:

- 1 tbsp. of olive oil
- 1 large onion, chopped
- 3 large carrots (chopped medium)
- 3 stalks celery, chopped
- 1 sprig fresh rosemary (minced)
- 4 sprigs fresh thyme
- 16 oz. dried white beans
- 8 cups of chicken stock
- 1 tsp. of fresh rosemary, chopped
- 2 cups of butternut squash, diced
- 4 garlic cloves, sliced
- Salt & pepper to taste
- 4 cups of swiss chard leaves, chopped
- Extra 1 to 2 cups of chicken stock for thinning soup
- ½ cup of sour cream
- 1 cup of crouton

Cooking Instructions:

1. Select the Sauté function and preheat the Instant Pot. Add in the olive oil. Once hot, Sauté the onion, celery and carrot in it until delicate.

2. Add in the white beans, rosemary sprig, thyme sprig, chicken stock and pepper to pot

3. Secure the Lid and make sure vent is closed. Select the Bean/Chili function, set to cook at High Pressure for about 35 minutes.

4. When the time is up, do a quick pressure release and remove the Lid carefully.

5. Add the butternut squash, garlic, crisp rosemary, garlic and salt and pepper. Secure the Lid and make sure vent is closed.

6. Select the Manual function, set to cook at High Pressure for about 10 minutes.

7. When the time is up, allow it to release pressure naturally. Remove the Lid and Stir in the chard greens just before serving.

8. Use staying chicken stock to thin soup if too thick. Pull out the stems of rosemary and thyme.

9. Taste and season with salt if necessary. Serve with a spot of acrid cream and bread garnishes.

10. Serve and enjoy.

Navy Bean Soup

Preparation time: 10 minutes
Cooking time: 1 hr. 20 minutes
Total time: 1 hr. 30 minutes

Recipe Ingredients:

- 2 Cups of dried navy beans (sorted & rinsed)
- 1 meaty ham bone, 2 lb. ham shanks or 2 lb. smoked pork hocks
- 2 large potatoes (washed & diced, peeled or unpeeled)
- 2 teaspoons of salt
- ½ tsp. of pepper
- 1 large onion (chopped)
- 2 medium stalks celery, chopped (optional)
- 1 clove garlic (finely chopped)
- 2 cups of cooked and pureed pumpkin (or other winter squash)
- 7-½ cups of water

Cooking Instructions:

1. Add in all the Ingredients in your Instant Pot (do not to fill water over the fill line).

2. Secure the Lid and make sure vent is closed. Select the Manual function, set to cook at High Pressure for about 80 minutes.

3. When the time is up, do a quick pressure release and remove the Lid carefully.

4. Just preceding serving, remove ham bone, hack meat and come back to soup.

5. Select the Sauté function and cook-blend until the point that soup achieves a decent consistency.

6. Taste and season with salt and pepper if necessary.

7. Serve and enjoy.

Vegetable, Beef and Rice Soup

Preparation time: 12 minutes
Cooking time: 5 minutes
Total time: 17 minutes
Serves: 5 to 6 people

Recipe Ingredients:
- 1 lb. of lean ground beef
- 1 tbsp. of oil
- 1 large onion (diced)
- 1 rib celery (chopped)
- 3 cloves garlic (finely chopped or pressed)
- 2 (14 oz.) of can beef broth
- 1 (14 oz.) of can crushed tomatoes
- 1 (12 oz.) bottle original or spicy Hot V8 juice
- ½ cup of long grain white rice
- 1 (15 oz.) can garbanzo beans (drained & rinsed)
- 1 large potato (peeled & diced into 1-inch pieces)
- 2 carrots (peeled then sliced into thin coins)
- ½ cup of frozen peas (thawed)
- Salt & pepper to taste

Cooking Instructions:
1. Select the Sauté function and preheat the Instant Pot. Add in the ground hamburger.

2. Cook until the point that browned and evacuate to a plate fixed with paper towels.

3. Add in oil to pot and cook-blend the onion, celery in it until the point when the onion is delicate for about 4 to 5 minutes.

4. Add the garlic, and cook for extra 1 minute before adding the hamburger juices, tomatoes, V8 juice, rice, garbanzo beans, potatoes, carrots, and browned ground meat.

5. Mix well to combine. Secure the Lid and make sure vent is closed. Select the Manual function, set to cook at High Pressure for about 4 minutes.

6. When the time is up, do a quick pressure release and mix in the peas. Taste and season with salt and pepper if necessary.

7. Serve and enjoy.

CHAPTER 12: VEGETABLE/VEGETERIAN RECIPES

Sesame Bok Choy

Total time: 9 minutes
Preparation time: 5 minutes
Cooking time: 4 minutes

Recipe Ingredients:
- 1 cup of water
- 1 medium head Bok choy
- 1 tsp. of sesame oil
- 2 tbsp. of sesame seeds
- 1 tbsp oyster sauce
- Seasoned salt
- ¼ tsp. of ground black pepper
- ½ tsp. of cayenne pepper
- ½ tsp. of red pepper flakes

Cooking Instructions:
1. Add some water into your Instant Pot. Then Place a steamer basket into the pot and put the Bok choy in the steamer basket.

2. Secure the Lid and make sure vent is closed. Select the Manual function, set to cook at High Pressure for about 4 minutes.

3. When the time is up, do a quick pressure release. Transfer the Bok choy to a clean bowl and toss with the remaining recipe ingredients.

4. Serve and enjoy.

Mushroom Thyme Oatmeal

Total time: 23 minutes
Preparation time: 8 minutes
Cooking time: 15 minutes
Recipe Ingredients:

- 2 tbsp. of olive oil
- 8 oz. of crimini mushrooms (to be sliced)
- 2 tbsp. of cooking butter
- ½ medium onion (finely diced)
- 2 tbsp. of minced garlic
- 1 cup of steel cut oats
- 14 oz. /1 can chicken broth
- ½ cup of water
- 3 sprigs fresh thyme (additional for garnish)
- ¼ tsp. of salt
- ½ cup of smoked gouda (finely grated)
- Salt to taste
- ground pepper

Cooking Instructions:

1. Select the Sauté function. Preheat your Instant Pot and add the oil, when heated, put mushrooms.

2. Stir to Sauté and reserve aside. Add butter to pot, allow the butter to melt and add onion.

3. When butter is melted, add the onions and for about cook for 3 minutes. Then add the garlic and cook for extra 1 minute more.

4. Add oats and sauté for 1 minute, add the broth, water, thyme, and salt. Secure the Lid and make sure vent is closed.

5. Select the Manual function, set to cook at High Pressure for about 10 minutes.

6. When the time is up, do a quick pressure release and remove the Lid carefully.

7. Stir in gouda into oat and stir continuously to melt. The pout in the mushrooms too and season with additional salt and fresh ground pepper to taste.

8. Garnish with thyme leaves if desired. Serve and enjoy.

Palak Paneer, Indian Spinach

Total time: 19 minutes
Preparation time: 10 minutes
Cooking time: 9 minutes

Recipe Ingredients:

- 1 lb. of spinach
- 2 tsp. of oil
- 1 large yellow onion (sliced and diced)
- 2 tomatoes (diced)
- 5 tbsp. of minced garlic
- 2 teaspoons of minced ginger
- ½ tsp. of jalapeño chili
- 2 tsp. of ground cumin
- 1 teaspoon of cayenne pepper
- 2 tsp. of garam masala
- 1 tsp. of Turmeric
- 1 teaspoon of Salt
- ½ cup of water
- Paneer (use 1.5 cups)

Cooking Instructions:

1. Select the Sauté function, preheat your Instant Pot and add oil to it.

2. When heated put the garlic, ginger, and chili and Sauté for about 5 minutes.

3. Add the remaining ingredients except paneer. Secure the Lid and make sure vent is closed.

4. Select the Manual function, set to cook at High Pressure for about 4 minutes.

5. When the time is up, wait to cool a bit and put into the immersion blender, mash by blending and mix in the paneer.

6. Serve at room temperature and enjoy.

Pickled Green Chilies

Total time: 6 minutes
Preparation time: 5 minutes
Cooking time: 1 minute

Recipe Ingredients:

- 1 lb. of green chilies (slice with a mandolin)
- 1½ cups of apple cider vinegar
- 1 tsp. of pickling salt
- 1½ tsp. of sugar
- ¼ tsp. of garlic powder

Cooking Instructions:

1. Add in all the Ingredients into your Instant Pot.

2. Secure the Lid and make sure vent is closed. Select the Manual function, set to cook at High Pressure for 1 minute.

3. When the time is up, do a quick pressure release. Spoon into sterilized jars and cover the slices with the cooking liquid until the chilies are covered.

Ajiaco Negro

Total time: 25 minutes
Preparation time: 10 minutes
Cooking time 15 minutes

Recipe Ingredients:

- 1 lb. of russet potatoes (peeled and diced into ¾ inch dice)
- 5 oz./1 medium carrot (peel and cut and dice)
- 1 cup of frozen peas
- 1½ cups of canned fava beans
- yellow corn (use 1 large ear, shucked and cut into 6 pieces crosswise)
- 1½ quarts homemade vegetable stock
- Kosher salt
- Ground black pepper
- ¼ cup of minced cilantro leaves

Cooking Instructions:

1. Add the potatoes, carrots, corn, half of the peas, half of the favas. Pour in the vegetable stock.

2. Secure the Lid and make sure vent is closed. Select the Manual function, set to cook at High Pressure for about 15 minutes.

3. When the time is up, do a quick pressure release and remove the Lid carefully. Keep the pot open.

4. Select the Sauté function to bring soup to a boil and mash the vegetables using a potato masher until broth is thickened.

5. Add the remaining fresh peas and beans, simmer until well cooked. Add salt and pepper to your own desire.

6. Serve sprinkled with the cilantro. Serve and enjoy.

Brussels Sprouts With Mustard Sauce

Preparation time: 8 minutes
Cooking time: 5 minutes
Total time: 13 minutes

Recipe Ingredients:

- 2 tsp. of sesame oil
- ½ cup of diced onion
- ½ of vegetable stock
- 2 tbsp. of Dijon mustard
- 16 medium to large Brussels sprouts (quarters)
- 1 tbsp. of maple syrup
- Salt to taste
- Ground black pepper

Cooking Instructions:

1. Select the Sauté function, preheat the instant pot, add the oil. Once the oil gets hot, add onion and sauté for about 3 minutes.

2. Mix the stock, Brussels, and mustard together in a separate heatproof bowl. Put the bell sprouts into the instant pot.

3. Drizzle the syrup over it without stirring, secure the Lid and make sure vent is closed.

4. Select the Manual function, set to cook at High Pressure for about 2 minutes.

5. When the time is up, do a quick pressure release and transfer the sprouts to a bowl.

6. Season with salt, pepper to taste.

7. Serve and enjoy.

Jack-Fruit Sandwich

Preparation time: 10 minutes
Cooking time: 8 minutes
Total time: 18 minutes
Recipe Ingredients:

- 17 oz./1 can jackfruit (drained & rinsed)
- 4 toasted buns
- ¾ cup of water
- ¼ cup of diced onion
- 3 tbsp. of tomato paste
- 1 tbsp. of maple syrup
- 1 tablespoon of minced garlic
- 1 tsp. of oil (preferably, olive)
- 1 tsp. of apple cider vinegar
- 1 tsp. of vegan Worcestershire sauce
- ½ tsp. of yellow mustard seeds
- ½ tsp. of cayenne pepper
- ½ teaspoon of salt
- Powdered black pepper (½ teaspoon)

Cooking Instructions:

1. Select the Sauté function, preheat Instant Pot, add oil to it. Once hot, add onion and garlic to it and sauté for about 4 to 5 minutes.

2. Add in all the seasonings, jackfruit, vinegar, syrup, Worcestershire, and tomato paste.

3. Stir and add water so that the jack-fruit is covered. Secure the Lid and make sure vent is closed.

4. Select the Manual function, set to cook at High Pressure for about 3 minutes.

5. When the time is up, do a quick pressure release. Stir and shred the jack-fruit using a fork.

6. Serving on buns with cabbage.

One Pot Cabbage soup

Preparation time: 5 minutes

Recipe Ingredients:

- 1 small green cabbage (chopped into pieces)
- 1 med size onion (chopped)
- 3 tbsp. of garlic
- 2 carrots (sliced and diced)
- 2 celery (sliced and diced)
- Red bell pepper (1 piece, to be diced)
- Salt & pepper to taste
- 5 cups of vegetable stock
- 1 tsp. of dried parsley
- 1 tbsp. of cooking butter

Cooking Instructions:

1. Add in all the ingredients at once to the Instant Pot. Secure the Lid and make sure vent is closed.

2. Select the Soup function on your Instant Pot. Set to cook at High Pressure.

3. When the time is up, do a quick pressure release.

4. Serve and enjoy.

Italian Tofu Scramble

Total time: 19 minutes
Preparation time: 10 minutes
Cooking time: 9 minutes

Recipe Ingredients:

- Extra-firm tofu (1 block, to be drained, not pressed)
- 1 onion (half-moon cuts)
- 3 tbsp. of minced garlic
- 1 cup of diced carrot
- Broth (1/4 cup, preferably vegetable)
- 1 can of Italian-style diced tomatoes
- 2 tbsp. of jarred banana pepper rings
- 1 tbsp. of Italian-style seasoning
- Italian blend nutritional yeast
- 1 tsp. of cumin
- 1 tsp. of walnut oil
- Powdered black pepper

Cooking Instructions:

1. Switch your Instant Pot to Sauté mode, preheat the instant pot and oil to it.

2. When it heats up, add the garlic, carrots, and onion and stir for about 3 minutes.

3. Crumble the tofu in a separate bowl, and add the broth along with the peppers, cumin, tomatoes, and seasoning, pour into the instant pot, stir to mix.

4. Secure the Lid and make sure is closed. and close the lid. Select the Manual function, set to cook at High Pressure for about 6 minutes.

5. When the time is. do a quick pressure release and remove the Lid carefully. Mix in nutritional yeast and black pepper.

6. Serve and enjoy.

IP Veggie Soup

Preparation time: 5 minutes
Recipe Ingredients:
- 2 tbsp. of minced garlic
- 2 cups of chopped broccoli
- carrots, (1 large piece, to be sliced and diced)
- 5 red potatoes (unpeeled, quartered)
- 12 cups of water
- 1 cup of dry Great Northern beans
- bullion or dry broth mix (read the label to figure out the appropriate amount)

Cooking Instructions:
1. Add in all ingredients in your Pressure Cooker. Secure the Lid and make sure vent is closed.

2. Select the Soup function, and allow to begin pressure cooking. When the time is up.

3. Allow the cooker to release pressure naturally, remove the Lid carefully.

4. Serve and enjoy.

Veggie Chowder

Preparation time: 8 minutes
Cooking time: 8 minutes
Total time: 16 minutes

Recipe Ingredients:

- 2 tbsp. of butter
- 1 cup of chopped onions
- 1 cup of finely chopped carrots
- ½ cup of finely chopped celery
- 1 tbsp. of minced fresh garlic
- 4 cups of chicken broth
- 2 large baking potatoes, peeled and chopped
- 1 tbsp. of flour
- ½ cup of water
- 2/3 cup of milk
- 2 cups of chopped broccoli
- 2 heaping Cups shredded cheddar cheese

Cooking Instructions:

1. Select the Sauté function, preheat the Instant Pot and add oil to it when hot. Add the onions, carrots, and celery to it and sauté till tender.

2. Add in garlic and cook for 1 minute before adding the chicken broth and potatoes.

3. Secure the Lid and make sure vent is closed. Select the Manual function, set to cook at High Pressure for about 5 minutes.

4. When the time is up, allow the cooker to release pressure naturally, the remove the Lid carefully.

5. In a small separate bowl, mix 1 tbsp. of flour with 1 tbsp. of water to form a paste and stir into soup along with the milk and chopped broccoli.

6. Secure the Lid and make sure vent is closed. Select the Manual function, set to cook at High Pressure for about 2 minutes.

7. When the time is up, allow the cooker to release pressure naturally, then stir in cheese.

8. Serve once the cheese has melted. Serve and enjoy.

Vegetable Stock

Preparation time: 5 minutes
Cooking time: 15 minutes
Total time: 20 minutes

Recipe Ingredients:

- 4 ½ cups of water
- 10 black peppercorns
- onion (1 big piece, quartered)
- carrot (1 piece, peeled and sliced)
- celery stalks (3 pieces, chopped)
- 1 bay leaf

Cooking Instructions:

1. Add in all ingredients into your Instant Pot, secure the Lid and make sure vent is closed.

2. Select the Manual function, set to cook at High Pressure for about 15 minutes. When the time is up, do a quick pressure release and remove the Lid.

3. Place a wire mesh strainer over a large bowl then pour the broth into the bowl for the broth to sieve.

4. Discard the vegetable and set broth aside to cool. Pour the broth into an airtight container and store in the freezer.

Brazilian Feijoada Stew

Preparation time: 10 minutes
Recipe Ingredients:
- 2½ cups of vegetable broth
- 2 cups of dried black beans (soak overnight)
- spicy vegan sausage (1 piece, to be chopped)
- 1 cup of soy curls (softened in hot water for 15 minutes and then drained)
- onions (2 pieces, sliced in ring sizes)
- 2 large pieces of carrots (to be cut into ¼- inch disks)
- 1 piece of red bell pepper, chopped
- 4 tbsp. of minced garlic
- Dry red wine (use 1/3 cup)
- 2 pieces of bay leaves
- 1 tbsp. of cumin
- liquid smoke (½ tbsp.)
- Paprika (½ tbsp.)
- ½ tbsp. of dried thyme
- Ground pepper
- Cilantro
- Avocado

Cooking Instructions:
1. Select the Sauté function, preheat the Instant Pot and Sauté the carrots, onions, bell pepper, and garlic in a small amount of water for about 5 minutes.

2. Add the cumin, liquid smoke, thyme, pepper, and paprika. Stir for a minute and pour in the red wine, stir for about 2 to 3 minutes.

3. Then add the bay leaves, vegetable broth, veggie sausage, beans, and soy curls. Secure the Lid and make sure vent is closed.

4. Select the Bean/Chili function and allow the Instant Pot to cook. When the time is up, allow the cooker to release pressure naturally.

5. Serve topped with the above toppings.

6. Serve and enjoy.

Ethiopian Gomen Wat

Preparation time: 5 minutes
Cooking time: 7 minutes
Total time: 12 minutes
Recipe Ingredients:
- 2 cups of frozen collard greens
- ¼ cup of chopped onions
- 1 tsp. of minced garlic
- ½ tsp. of Turmeric
- 1 tsp. of salt to taste
- Paprika (1 tsp.)
- Olive Oil (1 tbsp.)
- Red wine vinegar (2 tsp.)

Cooking Instructions:
1. Add the ingredients in a heatproof bowl and cover the bowl with foil.

2. Pour in 2 cups of water into your Instant Pot, place a steamer rack in it. Place the heatproof bowl on the steamer rack.

3. Secure the Lid and make sure vent is closed. Select the Manual function, set to cook for 5 minutes.

4. When the time is up, do a quick pressure release. Add oil to a sauce-pan and heat it up.

5. Remove the vegetables carefully and Sauté in the oil for about 2 minutes. Add vinegar and toss.

6. Serve warm and enjoy.

Vegan Texas Caviar

Preparation time: 10 minutes
Cooking time: 10 minutes
Total time: 20 minutes

Recipe Ingredients:

- 1 cup of dried black-eyed peas
- 2 cups of water
- ½ cup of chopped cilantro
- 1 tbsp. of jalapeño peppers diced
- 1 cup of diced onion
- Roma tomatoes (2 cups to be diced)

For Dressing:

- 4 tbsp. of olive oil
- 3 tbsp. of cider vinegar
- 1 tsp. of ground cumin
- 2 tbsp. of lemon juice
- 2 tsp. of salt
- ancho chile powder (½ tsp.)

Cooking Instructions:

1. Add the black-eyed peas and 2 cups of water into your Instant Pot. Secure the Lid and make sure vent is closed.

2. Select the Manual function, set to cook at High Pressure for about 10 minutes.

3. When the time is up, allow the cooker to release pressure naturally. Remove the Lid carefully to drain excess water.

4. Mix all the dressing items together in a separate bowl and whisk. Add the vegetables to the beans and pour in the dressing mixture and give everything a good stir.

5. Taste the mixture and adjust lemon juice, vinegar, and salt if necessary. Allow salad to rest for at least 1 hour

6. Serve at room temperature and enjoy.

CHAPTER 13: BONUS RECIPES

Spiced Potato Spinach Lentils

Preparation time: 10 minutes
Cooking time: 30 minutes
Total time: 40 minutes
Servings: 3 to 4 people
Recipe Ingredients:
- 1/3 cup of uncooked brown lentils
- 1 tsp. of oil
- 4 cloves of garlic, minced
- 1-inch ginger, minced
- 1 hot green chili, chopped
- 2 large tomatoes chopped
- ½ tsp. of garam masala
- ¼ tsp. of cinnamon
- ¼ tsp. of cardamom
- ½ tsp. of turmeric
- 2 medium potatoes cubed
- ¾ tsp. of salt
- 1 cup of water
- 5 to 6 oz. of spinach

Cooking Instructions:
1. Add the lentils in a bowl and soak for 1 hour, then select the Sauté function over medium and add the oil, ginger, garlic, chili

2. Cook until translucent. Add the tomato, spices and cook until the tomatoes are tender.

3. Mash the larger pieces for about 4 to 5 minutes. Add the potatoes, drained lentils, spinach, water, salt and give the mixture a good stir.

4. Secure the Lid and make sure the vent is closed. Select the Manual function, set to cook at High Pressure for about 8 minutes.

5. When the time is up, allow the cooker to release pressure naturally. Carefully remove the Lid, taste and adjust the salt and spice to taste.

6. Add more spices or garam masala if desired. Garnish with cilantro, pepper flakes and lemon. serve over rice or with roti/flatbread.

Chicken and Brown Rice

Preparation time: 15 minutes
Cooking time: 25 minutes
Total time: 40 minutes
Serves: 6 to 7 people

Recipe Ingredients:
- 1 medium onion
- 3 clove garlic
- 2 cups of carrots, baby
- 2 cups of mushrooms, brown, Italian
- 2 cups of brown rice, raw
- 1 tbsp. of olive oil
- 2 ¼ cup of chicken broth, low-sodium
- 2 lbs. of chicken thigh, boneless, skinless
- 1/8 teaspoon of salt
- 1/8 tsp. of black pepper, ground
- 1 can (10.75 ounces) soup, cream of chicken, canned, condensed
- 2 tablespoons. of Worcestershire sauce
- 1 tbsp. of thyme, fresh

Cooking Instructions:
1. Select the Sauté function. While the Instant Pot is heating, dice the onion, mince garlic, and chop veggies.

2. Rinse and drain the rice. Once the pot reads "Hot," add the oil and sauté the onions for 3 minutes.

3. After the 3 minutes, select the Cancel function to stop the sauté function. Mix the veggies, garlic, rice, and broth into the pot.

4. Place the chicken on top, add salt and pepper, then cover with cream of chicken soup and Worcestershire sauce.

5. Add about 8 to 10 small sprigs of thyme on top. Secure the Lid and make sure vent is closed.

6. Select the Manual function, set the brown rice to cook at High Pressure for about 25 minutes and white rice for about 20 minutes.

7. When the time is up, do a quick pressure release for about 2 minutes. Carefully open the lid and remove the thyme sprigs.

8. Stir the pot to shred chicken and mix in any extra liquid.

9. Serve and enjoy.

Red Beans and Rice

Preparation time: 10 minutes
Cooking time: 43 minutes
Total time: 53 minutes
Serves: 8 to 10 people

Recipe Ingredients:
- 1 medium onion diced
- 1 bell pepper diced
- 3 celery stalks diced
- 3 cloves garlic minced
- 1 lb. of dry red kidney beans
- 1 tsp. of salt
- ½ tsp. of black pepper
- ¼ tsp. of white pepper, optional
- 1 teaspoon of hot sauce, we used Texas Pete
- 1 teaspoon of fresh thyme or ½ teaspoon of dried thyme
- 2 leaves bay
- 7 cups water
- 1 lb. of chicken andouille sausage cut into thin slices
- 10 cups of cooked rice

Cooking Instructions:
1. Add all the ingredients to the Instant Pot except for sausage and rice. Secure the Lid and make sure vent is closed.

2. Select the Manual function, set to cook at High Pressure for about 28 minutes.

3. When the time is up, allow the cooker to release pressure naturally. Carefully open the Lid.

4. Add the chicken andouille sausage. Secure the Lid and select the Manual function, set to cook at High Pressure for about 15 minutes.

5. When the time is up, carefully open the lid and allow the beans mixture to sit for some minutes to thicken the liquid.

6. Serve the bean mixture over a cup of cooked rice and enjoy.

Mediterranean Style Fish

Preparation time: 5 minutes
Cooking time: 12 minutes
Total time: 17 minutes

Recipe Ingredients:

- 4 white fish fillets, we used cod
- 1 lb. (500g) of cherry tomatoes, halved
- 1 cup of black salt-cured olives or Taggiesche, French or Kalamata
- 2 tbsp. of pickled capers
- 1 bunch of fresh thyme
- Olive oil
- 1 clove of garlic, pressed
- Salt and pepper to taste

Cooking Instructions:

1. Add about 1½ to 2 cups of water into the Instant Pot and trivet.

2. Line the bottom of the heat-proof bowl with cherry tomato halves to prevent the fish filet from sticking. Add thyme and set a few springs aside for garnish.

3. Place the fish fillets over the cherry tomatoes, sprinkle with remaining tomatoes, crushed garlic, a dash of olive oil and a pinch of salt.

4. Insert the dish in the Instant Pot with a long aluminum sling. Set the pressure level to low and turn the heat up high.

5. Once the pan reaches pressure, reduce the heat. Select the Manual function, to cook at High Pressure for about 5 minutes.

6. After the 5 minutes, allow the cooker to release pressure naturally. carefully open the lid and distribute the fish into individual plates, top with the cherry tomatoes.

7. Sprinkle with olives, capers, fresh thyme, a crackle of pepper and a little swirl of fresh olive oil.

8. Serve and enjoy.

MEASUREMENT & CONVERSIONS

Abbreviations

oz. = ounce
fl. oz. = fluid oz.
tsp. = teaspoon
tbsp. = tablespoon
ml = milliliter
c = cup
pt = pint
qt = quart
gal = gallon
L = liter
QPR = Quick Pressure Release
NPR = Natural Pressure Release
PC = Pressure Cooker
IP. = Instant Pot

Conversions

½ fl. oz. = 3 tsp = 1 tbsp. = 15 ml
1 fl. oz. = 2 tbsp. = 1/ 8 c = 30 ml
2 fl. oz. = 4 tbsp. = 1/ 4 c = 60 ml
4 fl. oz. = 8 tbsp. = 1/ 2 c = 118 ml
8 fl. oz. = 16 tbsp. = 1 c = 236 ml
16 fl. oz. = 1 pt = 1/ 2 qt = 2 c = 473 ml
128 fl. oz. = 8 pt = 4 qt = 1 gal = 3.78 L

Acknowledgement

In preparing the "The ultimate Instant Pot cookbook 2019", I sincerely wish to acknowledge my indebtedness to my husband for his support and the wholehearted cooperation and vast experience of my two colleagues - Mrs. Carol Newman, and Mrs. Nathalie Coleman.

Alexander bedria

19172218R00127

Printed in Great Britain
by Amazon